The Coronavirus Collective

The Coronavirus Collective

messages of love, light, & hope

COMPILED BY JEFFREY HOLST
AND JILLIAN SIDOTI

Published by Last Life Ever Publishing
Chattanooga, Tennessee

Cover Artwork by Brad Ball – bradball.com

ISBN 978-1-952745-00-3

Printed in the United States of America

This book is dedicated to the front-line workers, the medical personnel, the grocery store workers, the food preparers, the delivery drivers, and the other people risking their safety to hold society together. We appreciate and respect all that you are doing for us.

In your honor we have decided to donate 100% of the net profits from this book to a selection of charitable organizations that together are helping to feed the hungry, provide fresh water to the impoverished, protect the innocent from the devastating effects of human trafficking, and spread their message of hope and light to the world. (So buy a lot of copies! We have a lot of work to do!)

CONTENTS

JILLIAN SIDOTI

LAST LIFE EVER IN QUARANTINE

I am not going to lie. *(Aside: I always find it funny when someone starts a conversation with "I am not going to lie." Why would you lie? Did I do something to make you want to lie to me?)*

Ok. Let me start over.

Let me be honest with you. *(Oh my gosh, this isn't going well. Why wouldn't you let me be honest with you? Why do I need to ask your permission?)*

I am just going to cut to my point; I was excited about sheltering in place. Sheltering in place meant some serious down time for me in my own small brain. Expectations would be lowered. I needed some lowered expectations in my life. I was burnt out from work, from parenting, from volunteering, and the busyness of life. Also, it would be my opportunity to live out the Last Life Ever philosophy of learning and implementing habits to live the most well-lived life in every aspect of my life. For me, this meant optimal personal growth, professional habits, family health, and philanthropic pursuits. But let's forget about all the things I was going to do for a minute and focus on how sheltering-in-place was going to allow me to let go of many chores and inconveniences.

Here is a short list of things I was going to get to NOT do by sheltering in place:

1. Drive kids to school
2. Drive kids from school
3. Drive kids to activities
4. Drive kids from activities
5. Go to the gym first thing in the morning because I would have the freedom to workout at home WHENEVER I WANTED.

6. Wear actual work clothes.
7. Do my hair.
8. Wear makeup.
9. Yell at children to hurry up and get ready for school.
10. Yell at children to get in the car.
11. Yell at children to get their stuff ready for school the next day.

Basically, I would be doing a lot less yelling. For me, this was going to be the summer vacation where we didn't have anywhere to go. Oh, it would be glorious! I would enjoy my house, I would enjoy my yard, I would enjoy my pool, and I would enjoy my family. The freedom of being trapped in my house sounded amazing.

What would you do with all that time, Jillian? you ask.

As soon as I got to my shelter, my home, my abode, I put together a list of the fantastic things I would do while hunkering down:

1. Learn piano
2. Learn violin
3. Play board games with my children
4. Read to my children
5. Homeschool and teach my children amazing things
6. Workout
7. Eat healthy
8. Reorganize my home
9. Clean out every closet
10. Clean out my cabinets
11. Garden
12. Paint my baseboards
13. Do that 1,000 piece puzzle of Van Gogh's *Starry Night*

I was going to come out of this quarantine a better person. I was going to be svelte and healthy. I was going to be educated and so were my children.

My skills as a homeschooler will be admired by all, I fantasized. I was still going to work my job as an attorney from my new home office/school that I had created out of the dining room that we only use for Thanksgiving and the occasional Christmas Eve. I broke out the chalkboard contact paper I purchased for the kids for Christmas. It came with this cool little chalkboard pen which I could use to make all my amazing plans on our dining room wall where I hastily put up said chalkboard contact paper. In my neatest, bestest handwriting, I made a detailed schedule of daily activities.

I gathered the children 'round. "Kids! Look at this amazing schedule I made for us. It includes everything! School, praying, exercise, having fun, spending time together as a family, playing music, and learning new things! We will stick to this schedule every day and I even included 'free time' for you to do what you wish." All three of my kids rolled their eyes at me, even the four-year-old, but I persevered in my quest. I knew in their heads they thought, *we are just going to watch television and play video games. None of this is going to happen.*

I had the very best intentions with the utmost enthusiasm for my mission. In the end, here's what I accomplished:

I watched Tiger King.

Jillian Sidoti is a momma, wife, author, entrepreneur, lawyer, and #instafamous. She is on a constant quest to live her Last Life Ever with her podcast partner, Jeff Holst.

IF NOT NOW, WHEN?

Now is the perfect time to create the life of your dreams. When the dust settles on Covid- 19, our lives will be fundamentally different. This reality is not a bad thing. What many people perceived as "normal" and are scared to let go of, is in fact a toxic blend of greed, inequality, hate, lack, and more. All of those negative values fuel consumerism, distraction and addiction to fill the joyless void in life. All of this is at the cost of individual well being, as well as the health of our families, communities and the world.

And for what? So that you can have an arbitrary amount of money in your bank account for retirement (which probably wouldn't be enough anyway) and the hope that your health is good enough to do what you long dreamed of doing?

Our days are literally filled with choices. Some are relatively inconsequential but others have the ability to change the course of history! Sometimes, these choices bring joy, such as falling in love or moving to live on a tropical beach. At other times, the choices are forced upon us, like illness or losing your job. Whatever the cause, we are choosing to move *from* pain or *toward* pleasure.

Several years ago, my wife and I had to make a choice. I was spending too much time as a slave to an online travel rating service, doing what I believed was necessary at our boutique resort to ensure that our guests had an enjoyable experience, in the hope we would get a positive review. Thankfully, we got hundreds of them; but they came at a considerable cost and became a threat to my marriage. Something had to change. My wife and son were more important than the bottom line of a business.

In order to change your life you have to change your thoughts and surroundings. It might be as simple as your clothes or rearranging your furniture or even your physical location. So, we decided to go on a journey. Our first idea, while hiking to a local waterfall, was to "drive down to Mexico for a month." That thought rapidly grew into, "let's drive to Patagonia!" the southern tip of South America. And so our next chapter began.

After much planning, we outfitted ourselves with equipment and a truck with a rooftop tent, like the ones we had seen while on Safari in Africa. It was light and small to get to all of the off-road areas we wanted to explore. However, this version did not last very long. With a 3-year-old son, it was too tedious to pack and unpack and did not provide enough stability. So we opted for the luxury version, a 35' motor-home, which was great for stability, but way too big to get "off the beaten path". So we had a third go at it… We designed and built our own expedition vehicle, a 4x4 cab-over truck with a converted dry freight box. Outside, the truck is relatively inconspicuous. However, it opens into a custom tiny home with intricate design details. It's the perfect size for our traveling homeschooling family. Check out www.facebook.com/pdx2ptg for photos.

The purpose of our journey was to explore, re-connect, and enjoy time together as a family. However, after traveling for 7 months we realized that our true purpose was much bigger than just us as a family. Our purpose was to inspire & empower others to create the life that they want to live instead of living the life they feel they ought to live. We were working with volunteer organizations and giving back, we were "being the change we wished to see in the world" as Gandhi so aptly put.

Our journey started by going 1,000 miles the 'wrong way' – from Portland, Oregon north into Canada rather than heading south toward the goal of Patagonia. The journey of life is rarely linear, and this was a detour worth taking to spend time with my wife's family.

Since leaving Portland in 2015, we have driven over 20,000 miles across ten countries and bought an oceanfront home in Mexico to live in for two years. My amazing wife has had two incredible water births, one in Mexico and the other in Costa Rica (with our first son being born in the U.S., all five of us were born in different countries!).

Two key disciplines that have enabled us to navigate this journey across many countries, cultures, language barriers and even childbirth are resilience and resourcefulness. It is this same resiliency and resourcefulness that allow us to be relatively unaffected by the coronavirus.

RESILIENCE

When you enter into the unknown, there will be things that knock you off course repeatedly. We've had our vehicle break down, deep in the jungle of Costa Rica, where we hadn't seen any signs of humans for several hours. We have gotten stuck in the mudflats of a lagoon in Mexico, with our truck rapidly sinking and perilously close to tipping over. We have had our tires blow in the mountains of Guatemala. Every challenge has provided an opportunity to grow.

What we've learned is that persistence and perspective will carry us through. The setbacks taught us the value of being present in the moment, open to other outcomes, and to explore alternative ways to solve a problem.

RESOURCEFULNESS

Before we embarked on our journey, we had to downsize from what we thought we needed. Everything had to have a purpose and ideally multiple uses; otherwise, those items were dead weight. We got most of it right, but occasionally we'd face a dilemma.

The solar power doesn't work? Pulled over by corrupt cops looking for a bribe, again? The toilet is broken? When we discovered that we didn't have what we needed, or we needed to create a better result, we found solutions, sometimes ingenious, sometimes simple, so that we could continue on.

Additionally, we became acutely aware of our consumption. When you have to regularly fill your water tank or charge your batteries in remote areas with few resources, you begin to see how much you are using in a very different light.

Along our journey, our purpose and vision crystalized piece by piece like a puzzle. We uncovered at a deeper level who we are, and how we want to change the world around us.

LIFE 2.0

This pandemic is an incredible opportunity to recreate yourself and design life on your terms. I believe that this is the catalyst for making different choices. When looked at with a different perspective, this event is your golden ticket to design your "Life 2.0" – a life on your terms; a life where the people of the world come together to make it a better place for all.

How can we improve life on Earth for everyone and everything? The first requirement is to have the self-confidence to pursue your dreams. There is no certainty in life. This pandemic is showing us that circumstances can change. The question is are you equipped to handle the changes that life throws at you?

Next, ask yourself, are you living your life's purpose? Do you wish to create a legacy? Maybe your purpose is hazy, or you have no idea; perhaps it's crystal clear. The important thing is that you recognize you are facing a choice. Are you willing to commit to take action?

On our journey, we started building Inspired Life Adventures, a transformational travel website empowering professionals who are unfulfilled with life and searching for more, to uncover their true potential through transformative travel experiences. Just as we were about to launch the website, the coronavirus hit. With travel restricted and people staying home in isolation, the timing couldn't have been worse.

But, as we have learned in our travels, there is an opportunity in obstacles. We are taking this time to work on refining our mission, to build additional systems, and to create a community to help those who have wanderlust but can't move around. And although we are isolated from others, we can still go into nature to explore, to rejuvenate, and to find solace.

If you don't know what your purpose is, or how to create something during this time, look for experiences that will help you uncover who you truly are, what you bring to the world. When the restrictions we face right now lift, explore. The world will have changed, and you will not be able to go back to being the same person. So, see the world through a different lens. What you see will give you a different view of yourself as well.

My invitation to you is to step away from the current fear, fueled by the pandemic and allow yourself to connect with something that lights up your soul. Do something so compelling that it lifts you out of bed in the morning to act on it.

FALLING IN LOVE WITH THE TREES

We want humanity to re-connect to the rhythm of nature and fall in love with trees. Why, you might ask? The forests are the lungs of the planet and we are destroying them. Isn't it ironic that the pandemic is a respiratory virus? We are violating our planet through overconsumption and excess waste. Pathogens in any system arise from that system being out of balance; Mother Nature has a way of righting what is wrong.

Another step needed is to separate needs from wants, conserve our resources, and find ways to improve life for all, as we are all one. Our culture wastes resources on products that don't need to exist. We waste time, effort, and mental energy designing, producing, marketing, and distributing things that don't solve a problem, are of such poor quality or they are designed to fail, so you consume more.

You may believe that you can't make the necessary changes on your own, you're probably right. This is the time to work together, we need to open our hearts and minds and start seeing possible collaborations, and to "fall in love with the problem!" Don't be drawn into the competitive trap of needing your solution to be 'better' than someone else's. Focus on solving the problem as efficiently and effectively as you possibly can. If we focus on our solution, we are egoically attached to it and this compromises our ability to solve the problem.

So Where Do I Start?

Start by creating a clear image of how the world will be positively impacted by the work that you are doing and then decide what will be your first step.

For example, my family and I are going to plant 1 million trees in Costa Rica! Our first step is to buy a 108-acre farm in the Cloud Forest of Costa Rica and start planting. The primary objective is to tackle climate change. But other significant benefits include reduce global CO_2, increased wildlife habitat, creation of wildlife corridors, as well as soil and water conservation. The primary reason for planting in the tropics is that trees sequester carbon faster due to the continuous growing season.

On this property, we will be creating a family-friendly community for socially conscious entrepreneurs who would like to contribute to projects, explore sustainability options for housing, and design financial security into an agroforestry model.

We are also buying an additional 42 acres of primary and secondary forest on the Pacific Ocean, where, immersed in nature, you can awaken to howler monkeys, be mesmerized by toucans and the majestic scarlet macaws, and watch humpback whales nurture their young in the bay below. The resulting retreat center will have luxury tree-houses with various platforms and elevated walkways through the canopy, trails along the forest floor or bathe in one of the various waterfalls. There will be places for inspiration and reflection, as well as fun activities like zip-lining to the central platform for yoga or your retreat! The center will also serve as a seed bank for future reforestation programs.

The next step is to begin the ripples...

We want to explore ways for families to reconnect with themselves in nature, to learn to respect their surroundings, grow food, and explore ways to live in harmony with the natural world. We want to support employment opportunities for local communities, and to contribute to education, research, seed collection, planting, etc. while hiring locals to build and maintain our vision.

Act as stewards for the land while providing opportunities to neighboring farmers so that they escape the stranglehold of the large agrichemical giants. We will organize tree plantations for local schools, where the children can freely enjoy the nutritional fruits and nuts from the forest to enhance brain development, giving them the best possible start to their lives.

There is no possible way that my family could accomplish this on our own. It's not about us; it's about raising the consciousness of the planet and evolving to live in harmony with Mother Earth. We are looking for collaborators, co-creators, funding, and support to start this movement.

So, where do you want your life to take you when you are free to explore again? That search could be in your backyard, in a new enterprise, or as a world traveler. The choice is yours. Wherever you start, now is the time to find your purpose, set your vision, and take action.

"Never doubt that a small group of thoughtful committed citizens can change the world: indeed, it's the only thing that ever has."
— Margaret Mead.

Pete Steadman is a freedom-preneur who's chosen to shape his work around his family. After having a successful career in the hospitality industry in his native United Kingdom, Pete found his way to Canada. Thereafter, Pete and his wife, Latisha, embarked on a journey from Portland to Patagonia. Pete has three children and holds a degree in Genetics.

JEFF HOLST

TEN MORE STEPS

Just after waking on the second day of February 2020, I went to my kitchen and swallowed an anti-malaria pill. Unlike most of the rest of the world (outside of China), I knew that my life was about to change. I had gone over my emergency supplies-antibacterial hand wipes, emergency food, more than a month's supply of medication, thousands of dollars in cash-I had it all on hand and packed. I was ready to walk out my front door and I knew I wouldn't be back until March.

That same day, the first Covid-19 death outside of China was reported, a 44 year old Wuhan resident died in the Philippines. I had been planning for this day for more than a year and had been thinking about it for a decade.

Later that day, wearing a backpack and carrying a large duffel, I was dropped off at the airport and checked in for my flight. I had packed and repacked my bags more than a half dozen times over the last few weeks. On my feet I wore barely broken in hiking boots that I bought to replace the ones that I had determined were a touch too small. The first leg of my journey was short hop to Atlanta. We landed on time but there was a delay getting to the gate and I barely made my connection to Amsterdam. I worried about my checked bag, which contained the majority of my gear including most of my emergency supplies. Another short connection and I was on a plane to Nairobi. My plan was to stay there a single day and then head to Ethiopia.

After landing in Nairobi, I descended the stairs onto the African tarmac. The late evening air was dry and hot. When I left my house only 24 hours prior, it had been a cold crisp winter afternoon. When I landed it was technically summer in the southern hemisphere. Nairobi is about one hundred twenty five miles south of the equator and sits at just under six thousand feet in elevation. I took a deep breath and tried to determine if I could feel any difference in the air. It seemed the same. In Amsterdam, as I had wandered through the crowded airport searching for my gate, I don't recall seeing a single person wearing a mask but as I climbed up the stairs and toward the terminal building in Kenya I saw guards wearing masks and checking passenger temperatures. I stood still as the Kenyan guard checked me for fever and worried about my bag and about my passport. I had been to China just a few months prior and I was afraid that seeing the Chinese visa in my passport might subject me to increased scrutiny at a time when I just wanted to get my bag and go to my hotel. I wanted to rest, it was already ten at night and I still needed to find my bag. I cleared customs quickly, they barely glanced at my passport and I was waived to the baggage claim only to learn that my bag was somewhere over the Atlantic en route to Amsterdam.

With barely thirty six hours until my flight to Ethiopia it was essential that I got my bag as soon as possible. I needed my food, gear, my toilet paper and my hand wipes. I distracted myself, the next day, by doing a quick tour of Nairobi. Other than several trips to Egypt, it was my first time in Africa. I had hoped to see some wildlife but instead saw a run down museum, a sprawling city, and an impoverished slum. I returned to the airport the next morning, the morning of Feb 5th and was relieved to find that my bag had arrived just in time for me to recheck it to Addis Ababa, the capital of Ethiopia. Upon arriving in Addis, I repeated the ritual I started in Nairobi, I paused briefly to take in a deep breath of slightly cooler, winter air. I had spent less than two days in the southern summer. This time the air felt different. I struggled ever so slightly to catch my breath as I climbed back up to the terminal building. I'd spend the next four days acclimatizing to new higher elevation. It was all part of my plan. I had a mountain to climb and needed to make sure I did it.

On February 9th, the very day the death toll in China rose to 811, officially surpassing the number of fatalities recorded in the 2003 SARS outbreak, my brother and Rick, a highschool friend, landed in Addis for a short layover on their trip to Tanzania. I joined them at the airport. We drank delicious local coffee and talked about how our world was about to change. The three of us boarded a plane and flew to Tanzania. Six days later, on Valentine's Day, around 4:30 in morning, I heard my brother climb back into our tent. We were camped at just over twelve thousand feet, three days into an eight day climb to the top of Africa. I climbed out of my sleeping bag and out of the tent. I stood quietly in the dark cold air and looked up at the peak of Kilimanjaro still more than 7,000 feet above me. I was worried. I had been struggling to keep up with the group. I drew in a breath and thought about the thinness of the air. I thought about the way it felt in my lungs, I looked down into the valley at the lights coming from Moshi town but mostly I looked up at the mountain above me. I was on a quest, for years I had wanted to summit this particular mountain. I am not a mountain climber, and at 12,000 feet I was already approaching the highest elevation I had ever been. I was worried I would get mountain sickness and be forced to return without ever reaching the peak but I was even more worried I would simply give up. The climb was much harder than I anticipated. I had known that the last push to the summit would be difficult but I hadn't fully understood how hard the first few days would be. By the second day of the climb, I had already begun to consider the possibility that I wouldn't make it. As I stood, alone in the quiet camp watching the day slowly approach, I had a choice to make. Later that same day, Egypt would report a single case of COVID-19, like me, the virus had made it to Africa.

Today, as I write this I have a choice to make. I can choose to continue or I can choose to give up. I can choose to use this time to better myself, to keep moving forward or I can stop and wait for it all to be over. No one would have blamed me if I had stopped my climb. My life would not have been ruined. I would still be me but I also would have known I could have done more. I would know that I quit. I would know that I failed. And so I chose to keep moving forward. I chose to push myself. I chose to keep making progress towards my long held goal of standing at the highest point in Africa. It was by no means certain that I could make it to the top. It was overwhelming to realize so much of my potential success was completely out of my control. It's not possible to know how many people successfully summit Kilimanjaro. Most tour companies claim success rates in the 80-90% range but it is commonly believed that the true success rate is around 65%. A significant number of those who attempt to climb the mountain but do not summit, succumb to acute mountain sickness, a potentially fatal disease that can cause swelling on the brain or fluid filled lungs. The risk of getting sick can be minimized but not eliminated, by taking your time, walking slowly, climbing high and sleeping low. The body needs time to adjust to elevation or it dies. Some people naturally adjust to elevation more quickly than others but we all need time to adjust.

That morning I chose to keep walking. Throughout the rest of the climb, I kept choosing to move forward. As people passed me on the mountain, and as my group waited for me to make it to camp, I continued to choose to keep walking forward. It was a thousand small choices that got me through that day and to the next camp. My mind kept telling me that I could stop. I could tell the guides that I had a bad headache that wouldn't go away, a classic sign of a high altitude cerebral edema. With symptoms like that I would be forced to descend quickly and more importantly I would save face. Getting sick and being forced to lower altitudes would not be considered a failure but instead a prudent response to a life threatening illness. I wanted to quit and I knew that I could fake the symptoms necessary to save myself the shame while doing it, but I also wanted to make it to the top. I wanted to prove to myself that I could do it. I had a choice to make and I chose to keep walking.

On February 16th around 6 PM, I was awoken when our guide opened our tent to check on my brother. He had been wheezing and coughing since the previous night and they were monitoring his O2 stat. After lunch that day when we went to our tents to rest (we would begin the final push to the summit that evening with the hope to be on the crater rim of the great volcano in time for sunrise), my O2 stat was in the mid 80s, low but not outside of the normal range for someone camped above 16,000 feet. My brother's O2 stat had been in the low 70s, when they woke him it was in the mid 50s, a dangerously low level that meant he needed to descend immediately. He would not be summiting but he also did not fail. He had pushed himself beyond his body's limit. Later, while recuperating in the hospital he would be told in no uncertain terms that if he had attempted to continue he would have died. While he was getting ready to leave and head down, I asked him if he wanted me to descend with him and he told me to go back to sleep.

I was worried about my brother, I was worried that I would give up. I was not able to sleep and at nine that evening, having gotten only a couple hours of sleep, exhausted and already struggling to catch my breath, I climbed into my layers. I hadn't showered in 7 days. My fleeces stunk but I barely noticed them as I layered one on top of another. I slipped into my snow pants, put on my down jacket and my rain coat. I climbed out of my tent and stumbled over to the mess tent for a cup of coffee. The plan was for me, a single guide and summit porter to leave two hours ahead of the rest of the group in the hopes that the three of them and I would end up reaching the crater rim at approximately sunrise.

Precisely at ten, my guide, Ponse, my personal summit porter, Baltius and I left camp and began to climb. It took me until 8:11 am to reach the summit. Enroute I had been passed by dozens of climbers who had started after me, the rest of my group caught up with me and passed me around 5:00 am. I so badly wanted to quit. My feet were aching (I ended up losing both of my big toe nails), my legs felt as if they could no longer move. I was freezing cold and sweating, as we zigged and zagged up the dark mountain, my headlamp illuminating the path, I would look only to the next corner and think to myself, "you can do this, it's only ten more feet." I stumbled and staggered. And finally after what seemed like hours I would reach that next corner. I'd lean on my trekking poles, close my eyes and take a micro nap. On one of these short rest breaks, I fell completely asleep while still standing up. Baltius, who spoke almost no English, came up behind me and softly played his harmonica. I woke up to the music, looked ahead at the next corner not able to see what lay beyond and thought "I only need to make it ten more feet."

We live in an uncertain time, we don't know what will happen next. We all have a choice to make. "Will we keep moving forward?" We each have to make that choice but we are not in this alone. I would not have made it to the top of Africa if not for Baltius and his harmonica. We need to find people to support us as we move forward. We can not see what is coming, we can only see the path that's lit before us, we can only see the next little bit, but if we keep moving forward, at our own pace, with the support of loved ones and our friends we will get through this. We are all facing an illness over which we have little or no control but we can take steps to minimize its impact and we can keep moving forward. "We only have to make it ten more feet."

Jeffrey Holst is a recovering lawyer and a full-time real estate investor. He is co-host of the Old Fashioned Real Estate Show, an educational show where the hosts drink bourbon old fashioneds and share real estate investing advice. Jeff is also the founder of Last Life Ever Community and co-host of the Last Life Ever Podcast with Jillian Sidoti.

DIANA GIPE

COVID-19 AS I KNOW IT...

As I sit and write this chapter, I have long time family friends who have been admitted to the hospital for Covid-19, the "Pandemic" our country is facing, they are fighting for their lives. I have family and friends that have tested positive for the virus and made it to the other side, they can speak firsthand of the mystery virus we can't see but all can feel. As I sit and write, the death numbers continue to exponentially rise across the United States, the place many of us call "home." My heart continues to be with them during this time because this is a fatal virus that has taken lives and has ripped not only family and friends apart but a country, our country, a place we might have thought was immune to anything like this. I honor them to find the silver lining in all of this and am mindful of this season and the harsh reality of this pandemic. I hope that I can encourage you to find what brings you the most comfort during this season, that we are not alone, we are in this together and together we will rise stronger and better for it.

The world came to a screeching halt and I began to finally breathe and heal again. See, my grandfather, the most influential person in my life, passed away December 21, 2019, just in time for Christmas. I was by his death bed until his final breath, the whole world was celebrating the holidays and mine was crumbling beneath me. I remember I traveled back home to Michigan where the world was still moving, at a fast pace, no one stopped with me to mourn. I couldn't catch my breath as much as I tried. I remember thinking to myself, *when will everything just pause for a moment just so I can process?* Little did I know Covid-19 was on the horizon.

I realized the world wasn't going to pause for me, so I poured myself into work, into escaping, into keeping busy, anything to just go full speed ahead, like the rest of the world. And then this.... This 'opportunity' to get my life, my heart, healed and in order. The distractions, they instantly vanished.

What if tomorrow all you had left was each other, then what?! Covid-19 has us stripping all the extras away and introducing us to ourselves and to our families once again. A reset, a fresh start, a pause; a pause button that just maybe we all really needed. See, we are not social distancing from each other but getting closer together. I see families walking together at the park. Mom, dad, kids and even the family pet too. I don't remember the last time I saw people outside, enjoying nothing but each other. I see the memories and creativity and positivity having to come from deep within to make this not only something we live through but something that we learn through and that we give, for me, my kids a glimmer of hope.

This week, in Michigan, the governor announced school closures for 1.5 million kids. No graduations, no proms, no transitions, no back to routines and friends and beloved teachers. No familiarity waiting to greet them with open arms, after this pandemic. Those connections, those experiences, all they have grown accustomed to, snatched by this virus, too much to comprehend for these children. I have a little kindergartener who worships her teacher, who loves her friends and routine and has such pride walking up to the school each day with her backpack bigger than herself. Gone...for now.

When the world feels like the weirdest place and things are upside down, how to I tell her the news? What do I choose to do with this change? How will I encourage those around me? How can I be a part of the solution for our country and for healing?

I choose to close the workbooks for the day. Turn off the news. Put away the social media. Draw nearest to my faith and to my family. I choose to see this as an opportunity we might never have; to slow down, to be present, to be here... NOW. I choose to see how much my 22-month-old is enjoying having her sister home, hearing the giggles in the yard, seeing them growing together and not further apart. Seeing this as a blessing that mommy is home with them. The one place they long for me to be, always.

What if you don't have kids? What if you don't have someone you share life with? What if you are all alone and feeling lonelier than ever through this crisis? Then what?! Choose you. Introduce yourself to you again. Take this time to pause, reset, breathe and just be, be still. When will you have time to do that again, with the rest of the country?! Turn on some music, feel sunshine on your face, put away technology and don't panic when its easy to lose control.

Take a moment to get centered and come out of this pandemic with a greater version of yourself to offer the world.

Out of all of this I have learned how much more it means to me to build community with each other and connection not because you are in pursuit of something to gain, but because this is the time that we can. Face yourself, find a need, fill it and remember empathy and love start with you. To the mom and dad that have lost their jobs and have little ones to feed and clothe and don't know how they will, bless them with a trip to the grocery store. Don't ask, just do it. To the person celebrating their birthday not able to leave their home; make signs, drive by, turn on the music and wave with all the wave you have in you. The wave and smile that you bring them is worth more than any birthday party they would get otherwise. They long for that connection, be that connection. To the nurse, doctor, grocery worker, post office worker; those on the front line that must continue and choose to serve us because they want to. Find a way to honor them, to appreciate them, to really make them know how much their sacrifice means to all of us. It'll go a long way, I promise.

This is our opportunity to rise. To be better. To do better. To change from the inside out so that when we can all go "out" again and greet each other again. We are greeting each other in warmth, in love, in empathy, we are high fiving, and smiling and realizing that we will be kinder, we will listen more, we might just slow down and we WILL allow people to process, we will appreciate the down times because this is our down time now. Forced upon us; but in some ways, much needed!

There is joy ringing in the subdivisions, with kids home now. There are people coming together singing from their balconies, in countries across the world, celebrating the hard work of those on the frontline; bringing us to tears. Go outside on your porch and listen to sounds you may have never heard before, and if you don't hear anything, just sit and wait and the comfort of just being will overwhelm your heart because when was the last time that you sat and you were "just being?"

My hope is that you take comfort in knowing that someone prays for you too. That someone felt the hardest loss she thought she could feel before the world started to feel loss too. I feel like I am just starting to 'live again," what irony, what an epiphany that Covid-19, this pandemic, has brought to all of us. Unexpected, unwanted, scary, but in ways the reset we may have never seen coming.

Diana Gipe is proof that we all can have a second chance to get our lives right. Diana went from the grips of drugs and alcohol to the life of her dreams. She is eight years sober, the mother of two wonderful daughters and is married to her "love at first sight." Diana is a successful business woman who is passionate about pursuing people in pain and helping them find their own path towards a better future.

FRANK MCKINNEY

THE GIFT OF TIME

As told to Jillian Sidoti:
Before the world's current circumstance, the globe was spinning on its axis at approximately 1,000 miles per hour. The world is now at a standstill and we really don't know for how long that will be the case.

I ask, though, "What are you doing with this gift of time?"

This opportunity to take a deep introspective look at our mindset, our lives, our relationships, our faith, our future will likely never present itself again.

To me, this is not a time to think about how to make more money or to come up with some new entrepreneurial venture. For those of you who are in business, that would be a complete waste of time.

Because remember, once you get the mind right, the money always follows. This unique period in time is your chance to get the mind right. Also, if this period in time is torture for you. It's also a time to find out why that is so. I am typically a beacon of realistic optimism and even my own beacon was dimmed, a month ago. Just like you, I was scared.

I was fearful for my family; my daughter was quarantined for 14 days when we thought that she had COVID-19, and fortunately, she did not. I was fearful to witness a planet that was firing on all cylinders to come to an abrupt stop as if the planet's engine blew and the planet stopped dead on the race track. After 30 years in business, I have never witnessed such a thing.

But what is encouraging are the signs that public sentiment is shifting, because once public sentiment shifts, optimism will start to infiltrate back into this wonderful country of ours. In other words, there will be light at the end of the tunnel. My tunnel, just like your tunnel, is very dark right now, but I can tell you it's getting lighter. There will be a bright light at the end of all of our tunnels and that light will not be an oncoming train, but rather it will be the arrival of the early signs and stages of optimism.

So we wait.

What to do? As I said at the beginning, use this time to get the mind right. Your mind may currently be thinking:

How do I pay the grocery bill?

How am I going to pay the mortgage?

How am I going to pay the rent?

But the time is now to get the mind right, because we have time and we have a computer in front of us. We can apply for all sorts of assistance programs to keep your business running and family fed.

In my line of business, I sell very expensive homes on speculation on the ocean in South Florida. Few are coming to South Florida to tour ocean front property. The market and my business are at a standstill, and yet I still have to feed my own family. Even though I have savings, I do not want to use that, so I have taken the time to apply for the programs available to me. You should, too.

However, once you do all of the applications and we continue to quarantine, it's tough to find motivation, isn't it? Sometimes we just want to cry and stay in our pajamas all day.

Maybe you found motivation, but realize that motivation washes off and goes down the drain with the soap at night. As a species, as human beings, we are unable to stay motivated, so quit beating yourself up over the fact that you cannot stay motivated to stay on that diet, go to church to exercise, the list goes on. I often find motivation and then I lose it.

"Well that bums me out, Frank."

Don't let it.

We spend too much of our lives beating ourselves up over the fact that we can stay motivated to do something that we think is going to better our lives.

Maybe you are inspired.

I'm inspired to plant a garden.

I'm inspired to go cook a meal, as Shandi Fortunato wrote.

How about inspiration?

As motivation washes off and goes down the drain with the soap at night, it's even harder to find any form of inspiration that endures.

"What about inspiration, Frank? Oh, inspiration! That lasts a lot longer than motivation!" you may think.

You might read an inspiring book.

You might hear an inspiring sermon.

But unfortunately, like a bad sunburn, eventually, inspiration wears off. Gone.

Stop beating yourself over the fact motivation and inspiration will wane.

You know what changed my life? It is something that I think we all could use this time for right now: aspiration.

Aspiration altered my DNA.

Motivation and inspiration might help Ignite aspiration. But aspiration is a little bit deeper. Ask yourself while you're home in your PJs as you're getting the mind right, "Who do I aspire to emulate in my life? Who do I look up to? Who is that person that I would really like to put my footprint into their footprint and actually emulate, or copy, or absorb some of their DNA, some of their person into mine."

You're still going to be the unique individual that you are, and you're never going to copy somebody and become exactly like somebody.

I asked myself these very questions to find aspiration. I didn't have the benefit of going to college. I also went to four high schools in four years. I had a lot of work to do to find a light to look up to, to find someone to pattern.

So who will you aspire to be?

This is the fun part, and the entity that you aspire to emulate doesn't even have to be a real person.

When I was younger, I loved playing Robin Hood in the forest of Indiana.

To me, Robin Hood stood for taking from the rich and giving to the poor. That excited me. I would strap on my little plastic bow and arrow and would go out with my friends who acted as my band of merry men.

But it wasn't the bow and arrow that excited me. It was the concept that there was a superhero named Robin Hood. I loved taking from the rich and giving to the poor.

I aspired to be like Robin Hood. Before we end, I will tell you how that aspiration came true for me.

I sell houses on the ocean in Palm Beach County on speculation, there are only about 50,000 people in the world out of a population of nearly 8 billion that can afford to purchase the homes I build. The average price of the homes I sell is $14.5 million. I buy the land, I build a house, and I furnish the home with attention to all the details. I put a For Sale sign up and hope, like Field of Dreams, a buyer will come. But it is not easy to market a product that has so few buyers. But this brings us to the second person I aspired to be as a boy: Willy Wonka.

When I read the book, Charlie and the Chocolate Factory, it was revealed to me that Willy Wonka was brilliant at marketing. Charlie and the Chocolate

Factory is the greatest marketing book of all time. He created a scarcity in the market to the point where crazy consumers were ripping through boxes to find the golden ticket. He created anticipation and intrigue. He created a frenzy. He lived in a castle that nobody got to see.

He was a very unique individual.

He was eccentric, but there is a fine line between the eccentric and the lunatic. The difference: the eccentric has the money!

He didn't just have money, though, he also had the best chocolate and the best candy. Willy Wonka did not cut corners; he was proud of what he was making. So, as a young boy, I absorbed a lot of Willy Wonka into me.

Two fake people, not even real, as aspiration. What made them similar? Risk.

No matter what you want to do, whether it is in duties as a parent, building a business, or tasks that are seemingly insignificant, you must embrace risk.

You must not allow fear to stop you from taking a risk.

After high school, I had no money. I had no connections. I had no education. I had no network. I landed in Florida with a $50 bill. At that time, I realized, to get ahead, *I'm gonna have to take a risk.*

I also had a real person I wanted to emulate that personified risk: Evel Knievel.

Evil Knievel was a daredevil, a stunt man, but more of a daredevil, a traveling showman that would jump a motorcycle over cars and buses. His first jump was over a cage filled with lions and cougars. He actually landed on the cage and the lions all got out. He had showmanship and a bombastic confidence.

Even though he was known for this risk taking, he would say, "I'm afraid. Every time I get on that motorcycle to jump over 20 buses. But I don't let fear stop me." I'll never forget that.

As we sit at home and we're afraid, wondering, h*ow are we going to pay our next bill and our rent and our children's medicine?* Don't let that fear stop you. Hop on that metaphorical motorcycle and jump over that impediment.

You might crash, you might get denied, you might go online and try to apply for an appointment, it might take days or weeks.

But you can't stop.

You see, we are all on some kind of roller coaster right now. When you get in that roller coaster and you're locked into your seat and they let it loose at the beginning. Then it slowly goes up that hill and your heart is pounding in your chest. You're terrified at the thought of what is about to happen. Eventually, you get to the top, where your fear peaks, but it is at this point, that you have complete clarity. You can see everything now. You're ready to dive down that first hill.

What happens when you take that first dive down the hill? Don't you get kind of excited? Doesn't that fear go away? Isn't that fear replaced with joy and excitement and thrill?

Have you ever been in a line to get on a roller coaster and you see people who get so scared, they just walk away? They can't do it.

Think of what they missed: that clarity at the top. Perhaps you were just as afraid as everybody else in line, but you get on the roller coaster. Then the fear subsides, it gets exciting, and then it's over. Then you will do it again. You run to the back of the line and do it again!

Fear is associated with a thought of taking a risk. Risk is almost always associated with a big change or a big challenge in your life. The world's going to be different when we come out of this. So if you condition and exercise your risk tolerance, like a muscle, your ability to withstand the risk, will grow.

I have experienced this tolerance and growth. After moving to Florida, I took a risk on my first real estate project: a $50,000 fixer upper in a bad neighborhood. I was terrified. I thought I had made a mistake as at the time, I had a great job as a tennis pro making over $100,000 per year at 21 years old. I risked that and all of my money to start in real estate because I realized there was a limit to how much I could earn as a tennis pro. Therefore, I moved from the tennis court into the real estate business.

How do we get to the point of embracing the risk that is before us?

1. Realize motivation doesn't last. It goes down the drain with the soap.
2. Inspiration lasts about as long as a bad sunburn.
3. Determine who you aspire to emulate.
4. Recognize that aspiration changes your DNA.
5. Contemplate the legacy you want to leave behind.

Have you thought about your legacy? It can be anything.

It can be a beautiful tomato garden.

It can be helping those less fortunate.

In my case, I build some of the most beautiful houses in the world. Those will be rubble in 25 years. That's not my legacy, it will never be my legacy. My legacy will likely be recognized by the fact that we've built 27 self-sufficient villages in Haiti, the poorest country in the Western Hemisphere.

We've provided shelter to 12,400 desperately poor children. These are children that were eating mud patties flavored with bullion and lemon juice. In other words, children, so poor that they are eating dirt.

I don't believe in a welfare mentality. I don't believe in an entitlement mentality. The system is fine, mentality is different. Our self-sufficient villages embody this philosophy. Each village typically includes 40 houses and a community center for sharing the Word of God, for community activities, and for schooling. The village contains renewable food sources, clean drinking water and some form of free enterprise. This is my highest spiritual calling.

My professional calling is real estate, but spiritually, it's providing for those less fortunate. This is how my Robin Hood aspiration became a reality. I get money from the rich by selling them mansions on the beach, and I give it to the people of the poorest country in the western hemisphere, Haiti, by building self-sufficient villages.

What is the legacy that you aspire to leave?

Keep your PJs on. We got another couple weeks or a month of this. These are things that you want to answer.

When we do come out of this, there's still going to be a lot of fear.

Our entire lives, we've been taught that we fear the unknown. As of right now, there are a lot of unknowns. To face these unknowns and fears, I think of a quote by one of my favorite philosophers, Anthony de Mello, from his book *Awareness,* "We do not have a fear of the unknown. What we fear is giving up the known."

We cannot fear the unknown. It is absurd. If you and I were talking and I suddenly punched you in the face, you wouldn't have previously been fearful of the punch because you didn't know it was even coming.

Despite this, most of us fear leaving the known. Right now. Staying home, being quarantined and cloistered is affecting our minds. What happens next? What happens when things go back to normal? We do not know, but we cannot fear that unknown.

Although this is not a religious book, there's a passage in the Bible that I turn to when addressing fear. Even if you are not religious, it is a great life mantra.

It is Luke 12:48:

"From everyone to whom much was given, much will be expected. From the one who was entrusted with much, much more will be asked."

You have been entrusted with a lot, even as we sit here in our pajamas in our homes. As the sun rises, how are you going to share your blessings, for God rewards responsible stewards and those who are responsible with their blessings. As part of your mindset work, you must believe that you have been blessed with the ability to succeed at some level, but that blessing and the blessing that come from that success are not for your sole benefit.

In getting your mind right, answer the following:

How will you share that with which you have been entrusted?

The authors and organizers of this book recognize they have been entrusted with certain blessings and have donated their time and resources to put it together. The proceeds of this book will benefit multiple organizations that support the poor.

However, the authors and organizers are not any different than you, in my book, *The Tap,* I discuss how we can all be tapped by God. The front cover of the book is the image from the Sistine Chapel where God is touching Adam, however, I removed Adam and replaced him with the silhouette of a man.

(Do understand that I had to pay a royalty to remove Adam. There is capitalism at the Vatican.)

The Tap teaches the reader how to recognize life's great tap moment. The cover represents how the hand of God taps the reader on the shoulder, how to recognize those tap moments, and how to act on those moments. The many authors of this book you are holding recognized a tap moment and acted on it. Their actions will benefit many people.

How about you?

I hope you've enjoyed my chapter. I hope you'll use this time wisely to get the mind right and realize the money will follow.

And remember: to whom much is entrusted, much is expected.

Frank McKinney is, a true modern day Renaissance man: Real Estate Artist, 6x International Bestselling Author (in 5 genres), Philanthro-Capitalist, Ultramarathoner, Actor, and Aspirational Speaker who sees opportunities and creates markets where none existed before.

Upon attending his 4th high school in 4 years (he was asked to leave the first 3), Frank earned his high school diploma with a 1.8 GPA. Then, with $50 in his pocket and without the benefit of further education, Frank left his native Indiana for Florida in search of his life's highest calling.

Now Frank creates real estate markets where others fear to tread. He has built oceanfront spec homes (homes built without a buyer) valued in the tens of millions of dollars, shattering price records with each new project. Frank started with a $50,000 fixer-upper, and climbed all the way to a $50 million oceanfront mansion – on spec!

Frank's latest creation? His FINAL $14M Masterpiece, 3492 South Ocean, that he just unveiled! Please visit his website at www.frank-mckinney.com

ERDENEBUYAN ENKHJARGAL

EXPERIENCING THE CORONAVIRUS FAR FROM HOME

I grew up in the vast, open steppe of Mongolia where the limits of the eyes form the only boundaries of the vistas and where the sky and land come together. There are no mountains, trees, or lakes to distract you and your thoughts, yet the sunsets are the most beautiful there. In the hot summer months, an endless mirage of nature would rise from the land and surround me as I tended our family's animals and protected them from wolves. I used to chase my little brother as if I were chasing him through an endless ocean, racing back and forth with our horses until day ending with the setting sun. I first read about the ocean in the book "The Count of Monte Cristo" by Alexandre Dumas and that vision of the sea was forever imprinted on my heart. It quickly became a lifelong dream to stand at the edge of the ocean. How lucky I was to have this book to keep me company when our nearest neighbor was several hours away by horseback. Yes, I was born to be free, ride my horse and race through the endless Gobi steppe. Now, I am locked in at the shore in Southern California, I am at the ocean I dreamt about as a child, on another continent, far from my beloved family and friends; the constant thoughts and dreams of my vast, free land have resurfaced in my heart.

I arrived in America in December 2019, planning to take an extended break from my PhD studies in Japan where I am researching the resilience of nomadic societies during times of uncertainty. Rapid socio-economic change and prolonged environmental events, like drought and desertification, are threatening this traditional way of life. Nearly 40 percent of Mongolians are nomadic. Grasses no longer grow and water is becoming harder to find. How little did I realize that the importance of resilience and adaption would play out in front of my eyes in one of the world's most powerful countries.

Mongolia is a land locked country, sandwiched between Russia and China. Our economy is primarily driven by agriculture; however, the fossil fuel industry is quickly reshaping the steppe to fuel the energy demands of its neighbors. Contrary to popular belief, Mongolia is not only a land of nomads, but Ulaanbaatar, the capital, is a bustling metropolitan city where approximately half of the population lives and works. The streets are lined with 5- star hotels, luxury shops, and fine dining. Many people, hungry for interaction with the outside world, speak English.

It was at the beginning of January 2020, when reports of the coronavirus spreading in Wuhan started to become a discussion point in Mongolia. At that time, the Chinese government had reported more than 800 cases of the virus and a few dozen deaths. Since Mongolia shares its longest border with China and conducts most of its foreign trade directly with China, Mongolian authorities quickly recognized the risk of keeping its borders open. Even before the World Health Organization declared the virus as a pandemic, Mongolia closed its borders, making it the only country after North Korea to do so. Schools were also closed, and public events cancelled. Air travel came to a halt, and anyone crossing into the country through one of the land borders we share with Russia was subjected to a 21-day quarantine.

In the first time in history, our president would cancel the lunar new year holidays, "Tsaagan Sar", Mongolia's most important day to celebrate our tradition and culture. Tsaagan Sar, which means "white month" in English, is a celebration to welcome the coming of spring, after surviving the long hard winter when temperatures fall below freezing for months on end. Typically, we gather at the homes of our grandparents' where we exchange hugs and kisses and check in on everyone to make sure they are doing well. It means so much to us, to our tradition and culture. During Tsaagan Sar, it is customary to dress up in our finest traditional clothes and give gifts to those closest to us. We sing songs, dance, and sometimes, the men and boys compete in a wrestling match to show off who has emerged from winter as the strongest. We recount tales from the past, usually rooted in the landscapes and environment, and show our gratitude for nature, the sky, sun, moon, and animals.

It was exceptional to hear that Mongolia would not be celebrating Tsaagan Sar this year, a direct order by the president in an effort to slow the spread of the virus. On the other side of the world, there was little I could do to help my family; however, I took solace in knowing that my nomadic family, so accustomed to a life of uncertainty and with no shortage of trauma, would find the resilience to weather the storm. Sheltering in place in California, I've had time to reflect on these traumas, and oddly enough, I've come to develop an appreciation for these times of struggle and crisis.

When I was a little girl, the summers were wet with rain. The land was lush, the hills would be covered in a velvet green and small lakes would form from the showers that occurred on a daily basis. As the youngest members of our family, my brother and I had the responsibility to look after the animals; nearly 200 sheep, 100 goats, 100 horses, 40 cows and a few camels. We would run barefoot with the animals through the lush Gobi grass, taking them to their watering hole. Other nomadic families would join us, as the seasonal lakes provided a much-needed source of water for all animals in the area.

In 2000, when I was 12 years old, our family cows became sick and one-by-one they started to die. Cows provided the main source of our dairy, and their infliction was a great disruption for our large family. Neighbors' animals were also getting sick. The government sent a veterinarian team to diagnose the problem. Within days the military was confiscating our land and digging large holes with machines like none I had ever seen before. I later learned they were excavators commonly used for digging large mines in the Earth. These holes would become the graves for our animals, each of which was shot to death in order to prevent the spread of this mysterious disease. I was too young to understand what was going on. But I was not too young to see that my father was crying alone out of desperation, having lost all his Livestock.

The following summer the rain did not come, and the land was not velvety green. The few sheep and goats that we did have were at risk, and my father and brothers had to move deeper into the Gobi to look for grasses and water for the animals, leaving me, my sister and my younger brother to look after the home. Sandstorms were a common occurrence, and our ger, the traditional white felt tent that serves as shelter for nomadic families, collapsed under the strong winds. During those days I had nightmares almost every night. That summer became the longest summer of my life. Every evening we would climb a small hill hoping to see if our dad and older brothers would be coming back with the animals. This routine went on for two months. We had almost no food to eat, just some dried meat left from the winter and a small bit of flour. I remember missing the dairy products, the fresh milk tea, butter, and yogurt, that we would have in better times. No rain meant that we could also not rely on the variety of wild Gobi plants like wild onion and radish that gave us sustenance. The only certainty was the constant red dust storms that would sweep through our camp.

One night, right before dusk, we saw two big trucks coming over the hill toward our home in the middle of the Gobi Desert. My brother and I were happy by the sight of people, but my sister was concerned. Was it our father and brother? The truck pulled up to the door of our ger and two men stepped out and approached us. They said they were government officials and they had come to give us one bag of rice, one bag of sugar, and one bag of dry milk as compensation for killing our animals. As a child, I was happy, not having tasted sugar in months. I will never forget that night, sitting around the open fire, sucking on spoonfuls of sugar, and talking about our beloved animals. I fell asleep to dreams of rain and the return of my father and brothers.

Unfortunately, the rains would not arrive that summer and our few remaining animals died from the drought. With few options, many nomadic families moved to Ulaanbaatar, in search of work. Many ended up living in the slums on the periphery, where there was no electricity, no sanitation, no water, no basic health care, no schooling for their children, and of course very few job opportunities for former herders who had no formal education.

Now, as I reflect on that period of hardship, I recognize it as not only a physical and economic battle against a changing climate, but it was also a huge mental battle, where we were forced to watch our traditional livelihoods perish right before our eyes. We were stripped of our income, our food and our sense of purpose. We had lost our identity.

Mongolia's nomads have been living in harmony with nature for thousands of years. We are taught to respect water as the source of life. We are taught to respect land as the source of our food. And we are taught to respect every living being as part of the web of creation. Even rocks, we are taught, have souls. "Do not take stones for pleasure", we are told, because those stones protect the soul. And everyone should leave the well with some water out of respect for the other animals that depend on it to quench their thirst. When we suffer from an infliction, we are taught to take refuge in nature, to listen to nature, for guidance and comfort.

Our elders would say the current crisis is the result of ignoring the wisdom of nature. They would say we are too disconnected from the Earth, we have carried too many stones far from their home. We are striving too hard, and too fast, for better ideas, better inventions, and better things, while failing to acknowledge the costs that were paid to get there. We care more about success, and less about our wellbeing. Our elders would say that the current crisis is the result of not caring: not caring about the environment, not caring about the animals, and not caring about each other.

While this time alone has been hard, I have taken comfort in the wisdom of Mongolia's nomads. I have been able to reflect on my place in the world, and my values. While we all share in the responsibility of taking care of each other during this time, let us remember that we are also collectively responsible for the Earth. The devastating fires that ravaged the Australian outback, the cutting of trees in the ancient Amazon rainforest, the mass extinction of the world's biodiversity, and the rapid acceleration of the melting of the glaciers - all of these are our shared problems.

While many of us may feel helpless in this moment, we all can play a role in the solution. We have seen how single individual acts of kindness have made our communities more resilient. Let us keep the lessons we are learning from this pandemic close to our heart, for in the future we are bound to confront another crisis. Standing together, working together, loving together as members of the seven billion inhabitants of this Earth, will give us the best form of resilience in a time of uncertainty.

Erdenebuyan Enkhjargal is currently pursuing her PhD from Doshisha University's Graduate School of Global Studies. She earned her MBA from Shanghai Ocean University in Shanghai, China. A native of Mongolia, Erdenebuyan co-wrote the scholarly article *Assessing Local Indigenous Knowledge and Information Sources on Biodiversity, Conservation and Protected Area Management at Khuvsgol Lake National Park, Mongolia.*

PILI YARUSI

MY GIVE

Gratitude is everything.
I get to…
Vision
Endure

GRATITUDE IS EVERYTHING

I am grateful for my health. I am grateful for the health of my Husband. I am Grateful for the health of my Children. I am grateful that as I write this I don't personally know anyone who has been called to God because of this Pandemic. I am grateful that those that I know to be sick are still with us. I am grateful that I am able to keep my children close and hold them. I am grateful that we have food to eat and clean water. I am grateful for my home and the comforts I have within it. I am grateful that my husband and I can still work from home and provide for our family. I am grateful for those who are on the front lines everyday. Thank you to the doctors, nurses, medical professionals. Thank you to the Grocery Store personnel and the amazing folk who continue to do deliveries. Thank you to the truck drivers and gas station attendants. Thank you to you who keep the world moving.

I could keep on going. My blessings are infinite because my mindset is one of Infinite Gratitude. I am thankful each and every day and I wake up and I let the world know it.

How do I take action to continue my blessings? I don't let the fear take over, but I do have fear. I battle my fears everyday. Here it is:

> Rosey wakes up one day, her head hurts and she feels hot and cold. Her Mommy says, "Sweetie, take this medicine." Rosey didn't mind taking the medicine because

it tasted like candy and it made the bad hurt go away. Her Mommy cuddles with her and sings her songs.

Rosey wakes up later and she has a hard time breathing. Her Daddy says, "My love, take your treatment." Rosey puts the mask on and the machine makes a big noise. Rosey isn't scared though, she knows the machine will make her breathe better. Rosey is just learning to spell.

She can spell the word ASTHMA.

Rosey wakes up one day in a place that is all white. Everything hurts bad. She has a mask on but she could not breathe well. Her Mommy is sitting down next to her. Rosey asks her Mommy for medicine to make the hurt go away. But she can't talk because of the mask and tubes. Her Mommy can't do anything. Rosey tries to ask her Mommy to help her breathe, to give her a huggie, but she can't stop coughing...

This is my nightmare. My daughter has asthma and she and her baby brother both had horrible colds as COVID-19 was breaking. My husband and I took action and decided to self-quarantine ourselves and our three kids a week before the shut down of all non- essential businesses. As I write this I haven't taken my children out of a 3 mile radius of our home... and that's so my husband and I can get our run in and get some fresh air. We stay away from people and they stay away from us.

I don't mean to scare anyone with this story but this is the negativity that enters my mind. And I know that you have had similar thoughts. How do I rise above this? First, I speak to someone. Then I need to take responsibility for my thoughts. I have a very creative and sometimes dark mind but I cannot let my negativity take over. Negative self-talk is the death of a Healthy Mindset. So I count my Blessings and I Multiply them.

I GET TO

How do you Multiply your Blessings? Make a list of ALL THE THINGS you GET to do. Here's mine:

1. I GET TO stay at home with my amazing husband and children.
2. I GET TO create an educational, enriching and elevating atmosphere

for my children to learn in and grow. I get to spend these precious days with them.

3. I GET TO learn something new. By educating myself and bettering my situation in life I can lead a fuller life.

4. I GET TO donate to causes I believe in.

5. I GET TO keep an eye on my friends. Even in this time of social distancing I will actively reach out to people I know. Maybe one of my friends is having a hard time dealing with the changes. Maybe the news has scared them so much that they are screaming inside even though they may seem calm. Maybe I'll be able to help. But I won't know unless I pick up a phone and ask.

6. I GET TO teach. I get to share my positivity with the world and teach others how to live a #fitrichlife.

7. I GET TO work. My husband and I keep ourselves going by thinking up new ways to get our positive message #fitrichlife out there.

VISION

In order to have clear vision you must be forward thinking. I never walk backward. I take sure and grounded steps. I look ahead to make sure I am on the correct path. This is my system in a nutshell. Constant and consistent forward movement. Sure and steady and self-correcting. I do not let my past define me. You must learn from the past and your failures and successes. Fail Fast and move on!

I do not let my future control me. The future hasn't happened yet so plan accordingly, diligently and do not dwell!

NOW: Say to yourself, "I am a gift to this world and I will be PRESENT!" DECIDE to take ACTION. Decide that your life will be better REGARDLESS of what is happening. Imagine a better life NOW. What would that look like? What gets you excited? How can you turn your passion into your life's work?

THEN: Ask yourself what clear, quantifiable, ACTIONABLE steps can you take to make your VISION a reality. Here is my vision and the steps I've decided to take to make it come true.

My VISION is to "Help others live Fitter and Richer Lives." My ACTIONABLE STEPS:

1. Lead by example. I focus daily on fitness and health not only for my body but my soul and mind.

2. Educate. I teach how to get into Large Multifamily Real Estate to those who have the drive to learn and implement.

What is your Vision RIGHT NOW? How will you live a #fitrichlife?

ENDURE

Be a SURVIVOR. Don't Just Exist. Endure like a Survivor. Even if the worst case scenario were to happen chances are, if you are: following the rules, minding social distancing, being clean and keeping healthy... you will survive.

So have a SURVIVOR'S ENDURANCE.

Focus on Positive Self-Talk. Negative self-talk is the death of a Healthy Mindset. Health starts with a Healthy Survivors Mindset. It all starts in your head. So take your Blessings and Multiply them.

If you are Healthy - make sure you STAY THAT WAY by eating right, exercising, meditating/praying, reading and journaling.

If you can Work - find ways to make money from home. Other people do it... Why not you? If you already have a business you can do from home... How can you UPLEVEL? If you are "essential" (Thank you for doing what you do.) then do everything you can to stay healthy. Have the mindset of, "The world is blessed that you are still working and YOU are blessed that you still have a job."

Take Action to Keep on being Blessed! You have choices. Take responsibility for them. What do I mean by that? You can choose to be and act negatively OR you can act with positivity, humility and graciousness. You can CHOOSE to put as much positivity into the world. You can CHOOSE to be receptive of the blessings that surround you. You can be that BETTER SELF everyday!

And don't forget to always GIVE. I have found that the more I give freely and from my heart the more doors have opened for me. When I give abundantly, I receive abundantly.

So grateful to you for reading. If I can help you in any way please reach me at pili@yarusiholdings.com or you can find me at The Jason and Pili Project on Youtube and your favorite podcast provider.

Books that have changed my life: "The Go-Giver" by Bob Burg and John David Mann. "The One Thing" by Gary Keller. "The Twelve Week Year" by Brian Moran. "The Greatest Salesman in the World." By OG Mandino. "The Miracle Morning" and "The Miracle Morning For Couples" by Hal Elrod.

Podcasts that are always on (shortened list): "Being Boss" with Emily Thompson and Kathleen Shannon. "The Gary Vee Audio Experience" with Gary Vee (explicit). "The School of Greatness" with Lewis Howes. "MFCEO Podcast" with Andy Frisella (explicit). "The Best Ever Real Estate Podcast" with Joe Fairless. "The Real Estate InvestHER Podcast" with Liz Faircloth and Andressa Giudelli. "Last Life Ever" with Jillian Sidoti and Jeff Holst. "The Jason and Pili Project" with my awesome husband and I.

Pilialoha Yarusi is the co-host of The Jason and Pili Project with her husband Jason. She strives for a #fitrichlife and her goal is to help one person a day lead a fitter and richer life.

Pili is a Wonder(Ful) Woman, Amazing Wife, Loving Mommy and Awesome Human. She has partnered with her equally awesome Husband, Jason, and created Yarusi Holdings LLC a Large Multifamily Investment Firm. She runs the Investor and Client Relations branches of both Yarusi Holdings LLC and Multifamily Foundation LLC. Multifamily Foundation is Pili and Jason's interactive education platform for investors to build a strong FOUNDATION with buying Large Multifamily.

Pili loves to play with her kiddos and husband, run, do yoga and crossfit. She and Jason have three awesome children and two English Bulldogs. Pili has her NJ Real Estate License and is a Realtor with EXP Realty.

JASON MILLER

WHAT WOULD YOU DO IN QUARANTINE?

Earlier today my friend Jeff asked me to write something about being in quarantine. And by quarantine, I don't mean the actual quarantine, but the lock down that we're facing in my state, and that people are facing in many States. Half the world population right now is in a lock down and a good chunk of the rest of my country will soon be in a lock down. The lock down here is going to last longer than many people understand, and we weren't prepared for it. I really haven't been doing what I should be doing here. The thing is I've actually thought before about what to do in a situation like this, although not exactly like this.

More than a decade ago I read a book about the Iran hostage crisis. When I describe this scenario, it doesn't matter whether I'm describing it accurately, because it's how I remember reading it, and that memory is what informs my thinking. There were many different Americans taken hostage in that crisis, and they came from different backgrounds and were taken hostage in different ways and in different places. There were U.S. Marines that were put in an actual prison, and they found ways of passing the time by replacing every expletive they could think of with the ayatollah's name. They would tell a guard they needed to go to the bathroom right away because they had to "take a Khomeini really really bad." What I've often thought of, though, is two Americans who somehow ended up being taken prisoner in something like a conference room--it's been a long time since I read the book. They were not in the embassy; they were in another place and ended up being seized there and essentially put under house arrest in the conference room in the building they were in when the radicals found them. They had a very small amount of time to prep for this, and one of the fellows grabbed piano sheet music from a piano in the lobby (he knew how to play the piano) and a Bible. These two diplomats were in the same room for many months of the hostage crisis and reacted quite differently. The one practiced playing the piano sheet music even without a piano because he could read the music and practiced it by just banging out his fingers on the conference room table. He made a real effort to memorize a lot of piano music. He also made an effort not just to read his Bible but to memorize the Gospels. And he worked out constantly, having a very strict regime. It was something like a certain amount of push-ups and situps in the morning a certain amount at noon and a certain amount at night. He took advantage of the situation to get crazy fit. His hostage mate, on the other hand, ended up very depressed—potentially brought on by his annoying roommate.

At the end of this, the one who sat around depressed had become very physically degraded and was just in horrible shape when freed. The one who took advantage of this isolation time thrived. When he ended up meeting his wife at the tarmac upon being released, he picked her up with his strong arms because he was now buff and told her that he couldn't wait to play the piano songs he had memorized for her and mentioned that he had memorized the Gospel of Mark or something like that. Something impressive. Again, don't take my words as an accurate version of this story—this is my memory of something from a book I read a long time ago. I don't think it's probably completely accurate, but this is the memory that motivates me. I thought about this kind of situation before, and well before we had lock-down orders. I told myself that if I found myself in a situation where I was trapped someplace and couldn't leave, I would want to be like the guy who memorized sheet music and the Gospels and did push-ups. In short, I'm the rare person who has actually contemplated how to approach a lock down.

Of course, I never anticipated that I would be in a lock down and that my day job would continue. The business of my job is unabated, but I really can't complain—I'm still getting paid the same salary I was before this all started. A lot of people can't say that. But even with work bugging me, I'm still getting to work from home. Everything else is canceled. I still have a lot more free time. And what am I doing with it? Not enough so far.

The difference between the two prisoners in Iran is that one refused to waste the lock down and the other let himself be depressed about it. Thinking about the prisoners made me realize I was wasting the lock down. I've been taking calls down in my home office / home gym but haven't been using the equipment. I've been scrolling Facebook and seeing my friends double down on their religious practice while I enjoyed not having the obligation to attend mass (and all the struggles with bringing the kids out). Rather than reading the stack of books piling up next to my bed, I was joining virtual happy hours. I was wasting a lock down. I'm not wasting it anymore. I've thought about what to do in a lock down, now it's time to actually do it.

My approach is to have manageable goals. A basic daily checklist. Unlike the prisoner, I still have a weekday-weekend divide.

Weekday
- Do my job, get it done, help the family as much as I can while working. Gym – at least a half-hearted attempt
- Walk
- Quality time with kids
- Try to help my son break his thumb sucking habit Participate in one daily activity posted by my church
- Pray the rosary or join my parish daily video chat for night prayer
- Listen to the daily mass readings or join my parish daily reading video chat
- After kid bedtime, either read or write or work on a small home improvement project

Saturday
- Gym – again, at least a half-hearted attempt
- Go somewhere to go for a walk with kids or some other kind of outing Try to help my son break his thumb sucking habit
- Participate in one daily activity posted by my church More major home improvement project
- Pray the rosary
- Listen to the daily mass readings
- After kid bedtime, quality time with wife.

Sunday
- Gym
- Family walk and/or play in the woods
- Try to help my son break his thumb sucking habit Liturgy of the word at home
- Family prayer and Bible reading Day of rest
- PE with the kids Pray the rosary
- After kid bedtime, quality time with wife.

Since I set this agenda out a few days ago, I've managed to stick to it. I see friends online whining that they're not getting anything done in quarantine or they're depressed—maybe even sad about not getting anything done. This makes me feel like I'm being more like the prisoner who took advantage of his time than the one who didn't. I feel good about myself and I feel like this is working. But the nagging feeling I get is—why didn't I do this before. Why didn't I stick to goals like this before. What got in the way of daily rosary or walks with my kids before? At the end of the day, we're all locked on this Earth for only so long—we're in this bodily prison for a set period. And I should live each day like that prisoner who took advantage of it.

Jason C. Miller is an author and in-house lawyer for a Fortune 100 company. He lives in Midland, Michigan with his five children and menagerie of pets.

KAREN MILLER

BEST LIFE EVER IN QUARANTINE

The other day I loaded all of my kids into the family SUV to go out for a picnic for what was our first full-family outing in a month. As we struggled to match shoes for the little ones and kids threw fits about getting in their car seats, I realized: I was living my best life ever in this quarantine. No piling the kids into the car, my husband was home. That morning I even received curbside vet service for my cats. They opened the back seat, took the cats, checked them out, and put them back in the car. This is working very well for me.

The COVID-19 pandemic has sparked a dramatic change in life for most Americans. Threat of becoming ill, rampant stay-at-home orders with a myriad of social and shopping restrictions, and schools shutting down have left so many Americans worried and wondering how to adjust their lives to function best in this unusual time. It is a time period we will note in history books. But while the pandemic has been incredibly challenging for so many people, it has been fruitful and bonding for my nuclear family.

A nearly stereotypical introvert, reading books, doing a puzzle, and hanging out at home are some of my favorite things to do. I stay home with my five young children, whom I homeschool. Our days are surprisingly busy; we school in the morning, do various household chores in the afternoon, and the kids have playtime after while I work on other household tasks and dinner. Every week we go to our church's faith formation classes (where I teach 4th graders) and swim class. And every other week, we head to a homeschool class in the fall and winter at the nature center. There's a relative rhythm to life.

Michigan's stay-at-home order upended the lives of most families in the state. Children at home and out of school, spouses working from home (or newly out of work) or facing working in higher risk conditions. There's stress and chaos. For our family, however, there's been relative peace. Much of life has gone unchanged. We still homeschool. And we still do household tasks. But we've gained so much. My husband is able to work from home, so we have no loss of income. And his presence at home is really wonderful because it means that we can see him more.

There are more movie nights and extended playtimes. Our days are simpler with no outings or appointments to worry about. I don't have to do the work of putting together a lesson plan for the 4th graders in faith formation. The children do not complain about their inability to go out; rather, they revel in the suddenly-spring weather that allows them to chalk up the driveway, jump in the trampoline, and to be chased happily by our rambunctious 8-month-old Golden Retriever. Walks around the neighborhood keep us moving and make that aforementioned pup tuckered out enough to watch Star Wars movies in peace on the couch. The walks also help to burn off calories from the bread I've learned to bake. For the most part, this period in time has afforded us contented togetherness.

Life in relative quarantine isn't without challenges. We have five-month-old kittens for which we struggled to get appointments with the shut-down of non-critical vet care. Food and household necessities, once incredibly easy to manage for our large family, are now purchased as we are able to find them. The store shelves are empty from supply chain problems and panic-buying. Our children do not see their friends. And we are unable to go to Church, a particularly sad deprivation at Holy Week and Easter.

Through all this, we can develop fuller and more positive connections with those closest to us. Communicating well, spending time together, sharing learning experiences in cooking or homeschooling all are things that could be done outside of a stay-at-home order. Perhaps, with this situation, families can learn the benefits of slowing down, curbing unnecessary outside activities, and focusing on that which is most important—those under their own roof. To read, learn, pray, cook, and play together is a gift to embrace, not a thing to do in small amounts of spare time. Through COVID-19, I've reaped some beauty in my family and hope others can find that for their own families too.

Karen Miller is a mother and home educator. She lives in Midland, Michigan.

ADAM ENOCHS

BACK TO BETTER

There is no question that COVID-19 has had a dramatic impact on people's lives across the globe. People from every community, state, and nation have been negatively affected in some way by the spread and severity of this virus. Though the degree of impact may vary from person to person, everyone is affected in some way. One of the most common questions I keep hearing, and I myself have asked is, "when are we going back to normal?" I think this is a fair question. Whether someone is observing social distancing out of respect for others, fear for themselves or loved ones, or purely out of obligation, it seems that everyone wants things to go back to the way they were before the spread of this global virus.

It's understandable that we desire to get back to the life we once lived before coronavirus. We miss going to work, we miss going on trips, we miss being in close proximity to other people, we miss going out to eat, we miss going to the movies, we miss going to sporting events and concerts, we miss going on vacations, we miss having people over, we miss shopping, we miss the life and freedoms that we enjoyed earlier this year. Though I also miss doing these things and believe we will resume doing them in the near future, I have decided that **I do not want to go back to normal. I want to go back to better**.

The simple fact is, there will be life after coronavirus. The question for most of us shouldn't be if we are going back to life after coronavirus, the question that should haunt us is what kind of life are we going back to? Being a Christian, there is a verse in Scripture that has resonated during this crisis. In the book of Romans, the eighth chapter and twenty eighth verse it says, "For we know that God is working all things together for the good of those who love Him and are called according to His purpose." I think this verse often gets misunderstood to say that all things will be good, but it doesn't say all things will be good. It says that God is working all things for our good. So how does this apply to our current reality of this global pandemic? As I said earlier, I don't want to go back to normal, I want to go back to better. I don't want to use this time of social distancing to sit on my hands, close my eyes, and just wait it out. I don't want my life to look the same as it was before this tragedy struck our world. I want to utilize this time to rethink, re-imagine, and refocus on what matters most in life so when we come to the other side of this, and when we go back to our lives, I won't be going back to the way things were. I will be going back to better than they were.

So, what does it mean to go back to better? This virus has made me refocus on two truths. Every single person has a purpose, and every single person has a limited amount of time to discover and live out that purpose. If I want to go back to better, I have to first determine what better actually looks like. I firmly believe that a person who is living out his or her purpose is living a better life than someone who isn't. If the key to going back to better is living out your purpose, then the first step to living out your purpose is to discover your purpose.

In Tim Enochs' book, <u>Every Day is Game Day</u>, he writes that, "Purpose begins to come into focus at the point where desire intersects with potential." So, what does that mean? Here's an exercise that we use at *Irrefutable Success University*. Make a list of everything that interests you, things that draw your attention, things that distract you, and things you're passionate about. Call that "List A". Then make another list of things that you are currently good at or could be good at if you put forth the effort. Call that "List B". Make a final list of crossovers or potential crossovers from List A and List B and call it "List C". Now, look at each item on List C and start to imagine how much better life could be for yourself, your loved ones, and others if you were consistently living out some of the items on that list. Obviously, there are some things that you might have the desire to do and the potential to do that may not necessarily be part of your purpose. However, this connection between desire and potential can be a great beginning point to help you discover your purpose. Pour over that list, think on it, rework it, sleep on it, and adjust it as you see fit. At some point, using this method will allow you to get a glimpse of what your purpose is in life.

Once you have done this, CONGRATULATIONS you have gone further in thinking about purpose than most people in the world! From this point, write out a purpose statement. Go through this same process of thinking on it, reworking it, sleeping on it, and adjusting it. Once you have nailed down your purpose statement, share it with someone you trust who will cheer for you and will also help hold you accountable to continue to live out your purpose.

Once you have discovered your purpose, think about the impact that it will have in your life as a whole. What areas of life are out of balance or may be holding your back from living out your purpose? At NEWLife Leadership we created a simple tool called *The Octagon of Life Assessment* that reflects a person's satisfaction in the eight areas that encompass a person's life. These eight areas are: physical, spiritual, emotional, intellectual, relational, vocational, financial, and recreational. Part of discovering and living out your purpose comes in the form of finding the appropriate levels of satisfaction in these eight areas. During this pandemic I have decided to rethink and refocus on what matters most in these eight areas and subsequently determine the necessary steps to take to increase my satisfaction in each of them. Success doesn't happen by accident, and if I truly believe that God is going to somehow work this crisis for good, I have to do my part.

During this pandemic I encourage everyone reading this compilation of perspectives to decide right now that once this crisis is over, you will refuse to go back to normal. Choose to utilize this time of social distancing to prepare yourself to go back to better. Think about what you're passionate about. Think about what you're good at or have the potential to be good at. Think about how these two topics might have a lot in common. Think about what your purpose in life might mean for you, your loved ones, and the world around you. Consider the possibility that someone in the world is depending on you to live out your purpose. What actions are you going to take to improve your life in each of the eight areas of the Octagon of Life? What are you going to do to make sure that when you step back into the world after COVID-19 that your intentions, your actions, and your life are stepping back into better?

Adam is the CEO of NEWLife Leadership. He earned his Bachelor's Degree in Business Administration and his Master's Degree in Leadership, both from Lee University. Since then he has had the pleasure to work as a team member at Chick-fil-A in Chattanooga and later directed the leadership development program at that same store. After his time with Chick-fil-A, Adam accepted the position of Leadership Development Manager with First Citizens National Bank and is currently with First Citizens. He met his lovely wife Whitney at Chick-fil-A while she was the Marketing Director for the store where he worked. They have been happily married since 2017 and live in Chattanooga, TN.

WHY I COOK

Every day, I work a 10+ hour day, come home and make a (subjectively) elaborate meal for two people. I'm always asked by friends how I do it. As a person living in New York City, who has the time or energy? Why not order takeout like everyone else? Why not heat up frozen pizza or a box of mac n' cheese? Ease the stress, they say.

But cooking, for me, is what eases my stress. I found cooking during a stressful period in my life and cooking gave and gives me purpose. It gives me a reason to slow down and focus on something that will benefit me, someone I often forget about during the whole work day. It's a practice in mindfulness, and that's one of the best things you can do to alleviate stress.

The knife moving across a cutting board, dicing root vegetables, is hypnotic. Hearing the oil sizzle as sliced onions and minced garlic hit the pan, filling the kitchen with that aroma, caramelizing to perfection makes me excited. It gives me something to look forward to at the end of the day. I get to feed myself and the people I love with nutritious food, real food— something hard to come by these days.

There's been a cultural shift away from real, honest food. Americans have become reliant on take-out and processed foods. We call in pizzas. We drive through a fast food joint. We pick up boxes of chicken pieces and disposable cups of mashed potatoes. We work long days. The solution is easy. It ends up costing us more (both financially and physically) in the long run, but the convenience, we feel, outweighs the cost. But for me, it doesn't.

Then, with COVID-19, the world around us came to a screeching halt.

I have encountered many people in the past three weeks who feel blindsided – no one has cooked in years and they forgot how. I've been asked how to hard boil an egg, cook rice, boil pasta, make a sauce, a soup, and, among countless other things, how to make bread. I'm a huge proponent of making your own sourdough. I'm happy people feel comfortable asking me even the most seemingly simple questions (especially when they could Google it). I love to help and wax poetic about the rewarding feeling of cooking a meal for yourself. It's a moment like now, a time full of stress, uncertainty, and anxiety, that we could all practice a little mindfulness.

I've been doing little cook-along-with-me videos on Facebook live and would love to share a recipe with you all: baked ziti. It is made with ingredients most of us have in our pantry, which is key during this time. Not only that, it tackles teaching two of the five mother sauces taught in culinary school: a béchamel and a tomato sauce. And to make a béchamel, you must make a roux. You will use these three things time and time again, for recipes unrelated to this. It's a homey meal that no one can say no to.

Grocery list:
Onion
Garlic
Carrot (optional)
Celery (optional)
Basil
Unsalted butter
All Purpose flour
Milk
Mozzarella
Parmesan
Pancetta (optional)
3 cans of diced tomatoes (14.5 oz) Tomato paste
16 oz of ziti, penne, or rigatoni

Step 1 (The roux)
Melt 2 tbsp of butter in a saucepan over medium heat. When bubbly, add 2 tbsp flour. Whisk constantly for a minute or so until well combined, but not browned.

Step 2 (The béchamel sauce)

Gradually add 2 cups of warm milk and whisk constantly until combined. Bring mixture to a boil. Then reduce heat to low/simmer. Stir occasionally and cook for about 10 minutes. Mixture will continue to thicken. The roux is done when it coats the back of a spoon. Remove from heat and add 1+ cups of shredded parmesan. Mix well and leave to cool. (If you only have one saucepan, pour this sauce into a bowl to cool. You'll need a saucepan for the next step.)

Step 3 (The tomato sauce)
Preheat the oven to 350 degrees (f). Dice onion, carrot, and celery. Heat a sauce-pan over medium heat. Add olive oil. Add pancetta and cook until it starts to crisp. Add the onion, carrot, and celery. Cook for 5-7 minutes, until vegetables begin to soften. Mince garlic and add to the pancetta/veggies and cook until fragrant. Add 1 tbsp tomato paste and stir to combine. Cook for 1-2 minutes. Add diced tomatoes. Bring to a boil, then reduce heat to a simmer. Add basil and cook for 20-25 minutes.

Step 4
While the sauce simmers, bring a large pot of salted water to a boil. Add pasta and cook for 5 minutes. Drain and add to béchamel sauce. Add shredded or torn up mozzarella. Stir to combine well.

Step 5
When sauce is done, add 2/3 of it to the béchamel/pasta mix. Combine well, but try to leave streaks of white. Put the mix into a casserole dish/cast iron pan/ oven safe pan. Put remaining sauce on top and then add more parmesan. Place in the oven and cook for 15 minutes.

Step 6
Remove from the oven. Place under the broiler for about 5 minutes. Let cool for 15 minutes before eating.

Shandi is a passionate, self-taught cook and science enthusiast. She is usually found experimenting in her kitchen, with her dog begging at her feet, in Brooklyn, NY.

STAY IN THE FIGHT

In the Summer of 2019, I committed to participating in Brazilian Jiu Jitsu training four to five times a week along with supplemental cardio and resistance training a couple of times a week. I've always had an interest in Jiu Jitsu out of my love for combat sports, particularly the Ultimate Fighting Championship or UFC as it is more commonly known. I discovered Brazilian Jiu Jitsu while serving in the US Navy in the late nineties. During that time, I watched a guy named Royce Gracie become the first UFC champion. His size constantly made him an underdog in most of his matches. They were truly "David and Goliath" matches because there were no weight classes in mixed martial arts back then. It was incredible to watch this small, thin Brazilian man go into a cage and force giant men from various fighting disciplines into submission. I was instantly hooked but I remained a spectator.

It wasn't until this past summer that I officially started my Jiu Jitsu journey. But everything was cut short due to a shoulder injury that I had been living with for years and didn't know about, a labral tear and partial dislocation in my left shoulder. During training I just thought I was dealing with the typical pains that come with aging and normal post training aches and pains. Ice and rest didn't seem to help, and I would keep going back to train each day until eventually my shoulder wore itself out completely and I had to stop training. This was August 2019. I was in constant pain and eventually I consulted with my doctor and an orthopedic surgeon. Once the injury was officially diagnosed, I then started down the path of physical therapy and pain management. I opted out of surgery. I made tremendous progress with physical therapy in a relatively short amount of time and I received the official ok from the orthopedic surgeon to go back to training at the end of February 2020.

In early March I picked up where I left off in my Jiu Jitsu journey although it felt like I was starting from scratch. My lack of endurance was showing after being out for so long. I decided to join a different gym instead of going back to my previous one to get a fresh start and perspective. The plan was to ease myself back into things. The gym that I chose is known for training amateur fighters that fight frequently on the local circuit here in the Dallas/Fort Worth area, real "killers" as they are called. I would soon find out that there was no easing myself back into anything which turned out to be exactly what I needed.

Being around high-performance people tends to bring out the best in yourself. I did make sure I wore a shoulder brace during each training session to provide added stability to the joint. Everything was going very well, I was meeting new people, learning new techniques, and my cardio endurance started to improve. But little did I know that everything was about to change, and my Jiu Jitsu journey would be impacted and put on hold once again.

A few weeks after I started my training, we were all notified that the gym was going to be closed temporarily to comply with a county mandate to shut down all gyms and non-essential businesses to prevent the spread of the COVID-19 virus. Like many others I had not taken the news of the virus very seriously during the weeks before. I had been thinking all along the virus was a problem in China and would be largely contained in that part of the world or could even be a hoax. I had a reality check when the closure announcement was made, and I was really devastated by the news. I had just started to get back into the swing of things in my training after being out for so long with my injury. I did learn a very powerful lesson before the gym closed and it came from one of the lead instructors. Little did I know this lesson would serve me in the weeks ahead. His message was simply "Stay in the fight". The message was given to me as I was getting mauled during a training session. This instructor wouldn't let me give up and he kept instructing me to "Stay in the fight" as he observed my struggle sparring with a more advanced partner. This lesson left such a profound impact on me that I recorded the moment in a journal that same evening. I am a person that rarely keeps a journal. Since then I have committed to make journal entries a habit. I have come to appreciate having a historical record to look back on and see my personal achievements and periods of struggle and the growth that resulted from it all.

Along with the gym closure more and more announcements came out at the same time including the closure of my kids' schools. My kids were about to wrap up their week of Spring break and return to school, so this notice was sweet music to their ears. Not so much for the parents. And not too long after that a stay at home order was mandated in my county and the public was asked to only engage in essential activities outside of the home including medical appointments and grocery and medication pick up. Social distancing and frequent handwashing were also stressed. I have three kids who individually are in high school, middle school, and elementary so these announcements made for an interesting transition for everyone. My kids have had to get accustomed to online school at home but thankfully my wife and I have been working from home for years so there was no transition for us to the online world of teleconferencing and we were able to offer some assistance to our children and assist in the transition. Some additional adjustments have had to be made as a family in our daily habits due to the uncertainty of food and supplies being readily available in the future. We are not living in fear or panic but we want to make sure we are doing everything we can at home so we can limit the need of having to go into public stores and risk exposure to the virus.

The initial shock and awe of my family's "new normal" produced a variety of feelings within me including frustration and anger. Early on I found myself focusing on the inconveniences of the stay at home order and pointing the finger at China and speculating on its role in the spread of the virus and all of the conspiracy theories to go with it. I started to go down the path of mindless internet surfing and wallowing in self-pity. I allowed myself to momentarily get bitter and my focus was in the wrong spot in the beginning. I am happy to say that mindset didn't last long. There is a quote that I absolutely love, "Ego is not your amigo." When my ego is in check, I can see clearly and focus on what really matters most. But when I let it go unchecked bad things tend to happen and life tends to become more complicated for myself and those around me. I had to remind myself that I have a family that needs me to be present during this time. I have a lot to be grateful for and the evidence is right in front of me.

Many people lost their jobs as a result of this pandemic. My job was not affected adversely, and I have a roof over my head and food to eat and my family is taken care of and we all appear to be healthy. I am grateful and don't take these things for granted. I have made efforts to check on my neighbors and see what needs they have, one in particular is an elderly widow and she was hospitalized two months ago with pneumonia so she is constantly on my mind during this time due to her high risk of contracting COVID-19. I communicate with her frequently and check up on her. She has no relatives in the area and sadly there are many other examples just like her.

I am sensitive to the fact that there are many people suffering right now from loss of loved ones resulting from the virus. Their lives will never be the same. Holidays and other special occasions will never be the same. I feel their pain as I have lost loved ones over the years including both of my parents.

My hope and prayer are that these individuals and families will be able to find healing and strength through all of this as time goes on.

I don't ever want to forget this moment in time and the lessons I have learned about myself and the people around me. I hope that when the stay at home orders are lifted and we're all back to business as usual that I demonstrate a better appreciation for things as small as a trip to the grocery store and being able to pick up everyday household items without interruption and delays.

In a blink of an eye life can be disrupted in ways never imagined but as I reflect on this period of disruption, I have found many things to be grateful for. I cherish the new friendships I have made as a result of this pandemic. I value my family and my friends so much more, and I look forward to the day of being able to reconnect in person. It is so nice to see people helping other people and providing a beacon of light during a time of darkness and uncertainty. I am renewed with a sense of optimism and I do believe we are all going to come back stronger and many good things will come out of this.

And as the future presents new challenges and setbacks, I hope my first reaction is always to move forward and not allow myself to get bummed out and accept defeat. There will be times where people will be looking for the calm in the middle of the storm and you will need to be that calm. You will need to step up and lead.

To go back to the lesson from my Jiu Jitsu instructor, when life presents challenges and disruptions, you "Stay in the fight". Don't get bummed out or overwhelmed. Help as many people as possible in the process. There are many things worth staying in the fight for. Your family is worth fighting for. Your friends are worth fighting for. Your health and well-being are worth fighting for. The elderly and those in need are worth fighting for. I have been renewed with feelings of gratitude and love during this quarantine period. Out of the chaos has come a sense of peace and a silent assurance within me that everything is going to be ok if I stay engaged and do my part. Things are not going to be perfect, life is going to continue to present conflict along the way and my path may at times be obstructed in the form of an injury, a storm, or even another global pandemic. But instead of letting these moments defeat me and break my spirit, I now choose to always let those words from my instructor echo in my head, "Stay in the fight".

Kevin Fox is passionate about family, Jiu Jitsu, real estate, and business. When he isn't working or attempting arm bars and triangle chokes on people, he spends time with his wife, three kids, and dog (Rocky) at their home in Fort Worth, Texas

TAKING BACK YOUR POWER

*"When you squeeze an orange, orange juice
comes out because that's what's inside."*
– Dr. Wayne Dyer

The same statement is true of human beings. When we are "squeezed" or put under extreme pressure, what we have inside of us is sure to come out. That could be anger, sadness, fear or worry. However, it could also be hope, peace, gratitude or optimism. It is our duty as educated and self-developed human beings to recognize our feelings and take full responsibility of our responses when we are under difficult circumstances.

The beautiful thing about COVID-19 is that it was able to give every one of us a very intimate look at the things we carry around inside of us. It has caused many of us to take a look in the mirror of our subconscious and realize we desperately need to restructure our belief systems. It has also granted us the opportunity to take a step back, reevaluate what we once thought was important and ultimately re-prioritize ourselves.

We all remember where we were, what we were doing and exactly how we felt as the news broke and the number of confirmed corona cases escalated. We all remember the emotions that were surging through us as our children's schools was canceled and work was either suspended or brought home. Do you remember the emotions this triggered within you? Was it a feeling of excitement or enthusiasm? Was it of peace and contentment? Or was it uncertainty, dis-empowerment and fear?

Our emotions are the indicators of our own vibration. The better feeling emotions like love, joy, ecstasy and freedom consist of higher vibrations while the bad feeling emotions like hate, anger and depression consist of lower vibrations. It is extremely important to be able to recognize these emotions as we are experiencing them. When unexpected circumstances like COVID-19 suddenly arise, it can trigger feelings that we have been bottling up over time. Our true power lies in the now by being absolutely present. Our true power lies in how we decide to respond to a particular circumstance. Through practicing self-awareness we can very deliberately chose how we would like to respond to all of the "curve balls" life might throw at us.

A true leader, when confronted with hardships, will lead by example. He will remain poised and inspire hope and goodwill through his own confidence, courage and compassion- all of which are high vibrational responses. His positive response in the face of fear and uncertainty will empower and uplift others. Not only will it generate a positive response from those around him, it will also immediately attract other positive circumstances to him through the universal law of attraction.

We live in a vibrational universe and everything exists as matter, made up of minute atoms that are in a constant state of motion. The law of attraction simply states that like attracts like. Essentially, whatever we think about it, we bring about; Whatever energy we are emitting is exactly what we can expect to receive back.

Therefore, high vibrational responses or expressions of love, enthusiasm and positivity will yield or attract people, places and circumstances that share the same high vibrational frequency of love. On the other hand, if we find ourselves involuntarily reacting to outside circumstances with anger, hostility and blame we are unintentionally attracting more low vibrational, unwanted circumstances that will certainly cause more gloom and doom both in and around us.

"As you think, you vibrate. As you vibrate, you attract."
– Abraham Hicks

We cannot always control the circumstances outside of ourselves but we can absolutely control how we respond to them. The first and most important step is to recognize any feeling of discord, any emotion of lack, and/or any fear-based reaction. Then we must identify why these undesirable feelings are inside of us.

More importantly, how we allowed ourselves to let these unwanted feelings take over in the first place?

It all starts with our beliefs. A belief is nothing more than a thought that you have chosen to accept as truth. It is important for us to identify which beliefs serve us and which ones do not. A belief that restricts or prohibits you from achieving your goals and reaching your full potential is a limiting belief. They are usually rooted in fear and a lack of self-love. For example if you believe that you are only capable of making $25/hr then the universe will support you in only offering you $25/hr positions. If you believe that your health is declining then your body will respond to such belief and sickness will ensue. If you believe you will never find the perfect spouse, you will then find yourself in relationships filled with lack, disappointment and incompatibility.

Our minds are filled with limiting beliefs that we have unknowingly picked up somewhere along our journey. We might have acquired them during a rough phase of our childhood, while working for a disgruntled boss or possibly from a trauma we experienced in a relationship. The important part is identifying what these limiting beliefs are and then dismantling them. Once we recognize them, then we can release and replace them with positive affirmations. As soon as we intentionally decide that we can overcome them, we will. All it takes is intention, focus and desire.

We all have "that voice" in our head that tells us what to do or how to think. Once we realize that we are not that voice and that we are the observer of that voice is when we can truly step into our full potential and greatest power. When we can change the narrative of that voice from victim to victor is when we will triumph!

When we take control and ownership of that voice, replacing our limiting beliefs with empowering affirmations, the real magic happens.

Thoughts have a frequency just like words have a frequency and the universe is listening and responding to all of it. When something good happens to you and you rejoice, the universe will respond by offering you more things to rejoice in.

When something unfortunate happens to you and you respond in fear and sadness, the universe will automatically respond by offering you more things to provoke fear and sadness. Kyle Cease coined the phrase, "And I love it!" He trained himself to innately respond with these enthusiastic words every time he was confronted with a difficult situation. He knew that if he responded in a positive way to a negative situation, he would immediately shift the energy and attract circumstances that were in alignment with his highest good, happiness and success.

> *"If you want to find the secrets of the universe, think*
> *in terms of energy, frequency and vibration."*
> —Nikola Tesla

When COVID-19 began to shift the landscapes of our lives what were our immediate thoughts and responses? We can use unexpected situations to analyze our own self-talk and create new empowering affirmations. Reciting universal truths can help you regain control of your thoughts, your words, your reactions and therefore your future circumstances. So even if you feel like you may not have control of a current situation outside of you, rest assured that by utilizing these powerful affirmations you can easily take back control of the future outcome.

"I know God is faithful and always has my back."
"I know everything is always working out for me."
"I know he always has and always will provide abundantly."
"I am strong and courageous."
"I am healthy and vibrant."
"I am love."
"I am joy."
"I am peace."
"I am ease and flow."
"I am harmony and wellbeing."
"I am abundant in all areas of my life."
"I attract wealth, resources and prosperity."
"I trust the process."
"I enjoy the journey.'
"I know that I am enough."
"I know that I am worthy."

There is a tremendous amount of power in these words. By stating these phrases and reciting them on a daily basis, not only will you start to believe them but your body will as well. Once you learn to embrace them, low energy feelingslike fear, hatred and depression will no longer be able to reside within you.

Consequently the next time a crisis rears its ugly head, you will only be able to shine bright, stay positive and pour out love and abundance to everyone around you. All while simultaneously attracting and creating a future composed of love and abundance.

In order to truly embody and embrace these affirmations you must first learn to love yourself unconditionally. Unconditionally means that it doesn't matter where you're currently at in life or what your past might look like. Unconditionally means that you refuse to judge, criticize or ridicule yourself or others. Unconditionally means that you are purposely choosing to celebrate your greatness, your divinity and even your shortcomings today in total self-acceptance.

Once you are able to truly love every aspect of yourself, you will passionately believe that you are enough and you are worthy. In total self-love and self-acceptance, you will allow yourself to make your wellbeing a priority. It is so common in today's society to put other people or things in front you, but the problem is that you simply cannot give what you do not have. You cannot pour from an empty cup. If you don't have love inside of you, how can you possibly be expected to give it to others? Like Dr. Wayne Dyer always said, "It's what's inside of you that counts." Learn to fiercely love yourself. Do things that fill you with love, excitement, fulfillment and joy so that way you can generously gift those things to everyone around you.

You will most likely notice that when you allow yourself to make your wellbeing a priority, you will begin to make choices, both large and small, in all areas of your life that will facilitate the fully empowered, best version of you. You will understand that you are worthy of investing in your education so that way can gain wisdom, knowledge and insight. You will be inspired to take action to broaden your perspective, network with professionals and strive to achieve your goals. You are absolutely worthy of dreaming big and pursuing your passion. You are worthy of investing in your health so that way you feel strong, healthy, alive and capable. You are worthy of positive and loving relationships that bring you laughter and joy. If you can take a stand for yourself today, the decisions you make tomorrow will not only benefit the highest version of you but also all of those around you.

Self-love and self-talk are very closely related. You deserve to treat yourself with respect and kind words of love and appreciation. Once you decide to stop any sort of negative or destructive self-talk in your head, you will certainly not tolerate it from anyone else around you. Self-love is intentionally raising the standard of how you treat yourself. Others will take notice and appreciate that you have decided to do this. They will realize that they too must treat you with that same level of love and respect if they desire to be a part of your experience. It is through your own love of self that you are able to attract more positive and satisfying experiences, people, places, relationships and circumstances.

Energy is contagious. Once you start feeling so good and in such a divine state of alignment that you cannot help but respond to chaos in love and appreciation, you will create a ripple effect. Not only will you inspire and uplift others around you in a spirit of faith and wellbeing, but you will also inspire the universe to continue to bless you with delightful and pleasing surprises along the way. The key to overcoming difficult circumstances is understanding what we can control. When we focus to make our wellbeing a priority, we will instinctively make decisions that fill us up with high vibrational energy. This ensures that if and when we are confronted with difficult or trying circumstances we will be well prepared to respond in love and a divine knowing that all is well.

Life is cyclical and there will always be ebb and flow. We will have our good days and our bad days, just like we will have excellent seasons and our off seasons.

What matters are not the circumstances that we find ourselves in; what matters is how we chose to respond to those circumstances. Dare to dream big my friends.

Dare to step outside of your comfort zone. Dare to surround yourself with people who are where you want to be. Dare to make yourself a priority and do what brings you true happiness. Dare to fearlessly pursue your passion. Know that you are fiercely loved, appreciated and supported. Life is a journey meant to be enjoyed.

Trust the process and listen to your heart.

Lucie Ptasznik is passionate about spreading authentic messages of love and positivity. She has been studying and practicing the law of attraction and meditation for 10 years. She believes that mindset, imagination and intention are the most powerful tools we can combine to create the life of our dreams. She loves to help people recognize and set aside their limiting beliefs so that way they can bravely step into their full potential.

MARISA WILKE

SLEEPING THROUGH THE INSANITY

Yes, I know, I know… you tried meditation that one time (or possibly more than once) and it "didn't work." You bought this book for a reason and I'm hoping you won't skip this chapter if this was your first sentiment upon seeing this portion of the book!

Many people have been feeling out of sorts with these unprecedented times that we are living in. Are you one of them? Welcome to your humanity! My only goal here is to help you with a few tried and true tips and tricks to help you feel centered and sleep better.

Stress is a normal part of everyday life. In fact, sometimes stress can be a good thing, causing us to get out of our comfort zone and grow. However, prolonged levels of stress can compromise our physical, mental and emotional health.

The current level of stress for some is leading to anxiety and insomnia. Has this happened to you? It's happened to me under stress, for sure! A night of missed sleep doesn't kill anyone, though it may make you a little tired and moody the next day. Several nights of missed sleep begin to affect the brain as though it has consumed large amounts of alcohol with impaired judgement and function. We begin to become short tempered with ourselves and maybe those around us (especially if we are quarantined with family). This can lead to increased amounts of caffeine to get or keep us going and possibly sedatives like alcohol to "take the edge off" at night. It can become a never ending familiar cycle of external remedies to an external situation.

If this is you or someone you care about, it's ok! I've taken prescription sleep aids prior to learning what I am going to share with you here. There are remedies to these problems that you have already existing within you! Your body is a natural pharmacy with everything in it that you could possibly need to regulate stress and sleep well. This isn't crazy talk! The latest neuroscience research has proven this. Your body makes opiates, natural sedatives, pain relieving and mood regulating neurotransmitters. Our bodies are beautifully equipped to deal with the onset of stress and the recovery from it as well. When we are healthy. They do not function optimally with prolonged stress. Are you ready to tap into your own natural pharmacy and inhabit your own temple of peace?

Right on, right on. Let's get down to it. The heart of it boils down to this: the breath controls the mind, the mind controls the body. Learn to control or work with your breath and you can learn to control your mind as well as your body! Ask any special ops personnel and they will tell you this fact! So what if you aren't special ops and you don't have the training they have? I'm going to teach you right here! You can become your own special ops force and master your breath in your own home without spending thousands of dollars.

Your breath is FREE. Your mind is FREE. What it will cost you is having an open mind, a small bit of discipline and the desire to become aware of the present moment. All of this is 100% free!

I challenge you in this moment to take a deep breath. Long and slow. Yes, right now. Put the book down, it will be here when you come back in a few moments.

Did you notice your shoulders wanting to come up to your ears? On the first try almost everyone naturally does this. I did the very first time I tried it! Did you also hear or feel the relief from your body upon exhaling? That was your body thanking you for giving it more oxygen!

Your lungs are responsible for oxygenating everything in your body as well as getting rid of carbon dioxide waste during exhalation. Did you know that most people only use the top 1/3 to 1/2 of their lungs when they breathe? This means that they could be oxygenating their brain even more for sharper thinking, and organs/tissues for top notch functioning and cellular growth/repair. Could you use sharper thinking? Better growth and repair means feeling rested and ready to go! Could you use that too? These techniques will do just that.

First, I'm going to go over a little physiology here to help you with this process. You are going to become well acquainted with the lower 1/3 - 1/2 of your lungs! Your lungs are enclosed by the rib cage to protect them. Your rib cage can be expanded by the diaphragm muscle in all four directions. Singers use "belly breathing" to strengthen this muscle so that they may hold notes for long periods of time on a single breath. Babies naturally do this type of breathing automatically which is why it can seem like an eternity when they let out a long cry!

As we grow older and experience stressors in life, our breath becomes more shallow and quick. Under stress our body does not know the difference between being attacked by a lion or a an email from your boss. What your body does know how to do is set off the fight or flight response in tenths of a second. Your breathing becomes shallow and your body releases adrenaline to hyper focus you for survival. Increasing levels of stress without a practiced attention to the breath means that your body believes it is in a constant state of survival, regardless of what it perceives the threat to be. Learning to train our mind and body to become aware of and practice this breathing is key to moving us out of a state of survival and anticipation and into the present moment. When we continue to practice we become really good at positively affecting our mood and sleep patterns. That's a great side effect, isn't it?!

Before we go back to the breath and rib cage, I'd like you to find a mirror to stand in front of so that you can see your belly move while practicing this breath. Facing the mirror standing from the side, I'd like you to inhale and stick your belly out at the same time. Create a "Buddha belly" or pretend for a moment that you are trying to make yourself look pregnant. Do two or three breaths like this each time extending the belly a little further, but don't hurt yourself trying to push your belly out too far! Remember that the diaphragm is a muscle and it may not be used to you expanding it this far...yet! It will! Now, try doing the breath the same way WITHOUT letting your shoulders come up so that the expansion is truly centered in the belly. Be patient with yourself as you practice this. Do this for 20 breaths and notice what happens.

Did it get easier? As you got closer to completing twenty breaths did your body settle into a rhythm? Please don't worry about focusing on the movement of the shoulder as a complete gauge as to whether or not you are "doing it right". You really will begin to know that you are in fact doing it right as you notice that you do in fact feel calmer and more centered than when you started.

Another way to practice this is to sit in a chair with your palms on your back, creating dual chicken wing arms, if you will. Practice the breath again like this for 20 more breaths, taking note of what we refer to as the "back body" in some yoga/meditation classes. How do you feel now? Pretty good? I'd be surprised if you didn't!

Let's bring the attention now to the exhale. Focus on the navel or belly button and bringing it all the way in towards the back of the body during the exhale. This does not need to be super forceful. More of awareness to pull the diaphragm muscle all the way back in to empty the lungs as much as possible. If you are overdoing this part, you will notice that your next inhale will feel the need to come quicker and the shoulders may begin to rise again. If that happened, no big deal. Start again. Remember that this is a practice of progress, not perfection. Now that you have practiced this a bit with me here, let's discuss when a good time to do it is for regular practice.

Upon waking and after relieving yourself is an optimal time to connect with your breath and practice this. Five minutes is plenty of time to start your day and set an intention that you will be aware of your breath during the day. We all have five minutes! This act could also be a discipline in not starting our day with social media, emails or work. Taking five minutes to breathe for yourself before making your mind, energy or emotions available to anyone else is a great way to show yourself what I refer to with my clients as "oxygen mask theory". During the safety speech on an airplane flight they tell parents to place the oxygen mask on themselves and then any children accompanying them. This is the same theory here. When you take this time with this small practice, you are honoring your body. You are honoring that you have woken to live another day. You are showing yourself that you will put the oxygen mask on yourself before others. What a great way to start your day! It is also a great way to end your day and begin to signal the body that it is time to sleep, restore and repair. Give it a go and see if you are able to drift off into a nice sleep, instead of with a racing mind.

That brings us right into our discussion of sleep. If you are a part of my inner circle, I will always ask how you slept the night before. It is a way of showing that I care and it also lets me know what state someone might be in so that I may understand where they are coming from and have extra compassion if they didn't get a great night of rest. I will share additional strategies that we can implement to aid ourselves into a beautiful state of growth and repair while sleeping.

You may have heard of these before, but reviewing again is always a great way to further wire good habits into our neurological systems.

8 Ways to Fall Asleep Better:

1. Limit caffeine intake (I recommend before 2 pm and two or less caffeinated drinks/day)
2. Time your sleep.

3. Stop screen time/blue light at least 15-30 mins before sleep
4. Bedtime routine (hot bath/brush teeth/cold room etc)
5. Breath Exercise /Meditation or Yoga Nidra, and/or Prayer
6. Rub your feet with oil for several minutes per foot
7. Herbs/Supplements/Tea (ex. Chamomile tea, Golden Milk, supplements not recommended by your doctor or health practitioner are taken at your own risk)
8. Be as comfortable as you can afford (mattress, sheets, pillows etc)

Limiting caffeine intake is always recommended to help anyone sleep better! It increases the heart rate and heats up the body, making it difficult to settle the mind and body for a good night of rest. If you drink caffeine (I enjoy a good cup of coffee!) lunch is the last time that is recommended to do so, so enjoy the beverage of your choice (please, no "energy" drinks...but that's a topic for a whole other time)!

Timing of sleep is HUGE! A sleep cycle is about 90 minutes. As we come to the end of a sleep cycle it is much easier for our bodies to be roused because there is a lightness of the brain waves at that time. So...what we have heard our whole lives about getting 8 hours of rest is sort of incorrect. Close, but not quite. Therefore, recommended sleep cycles should be 3, 4.5, 6, 7.5, 9, 10.5 or 12 hours of sleep. One should be so lucky as to get the last few! OR you can train you body to do so.

I generally sleep 6 hours 4 nights per week with one 3 or 3.5 hour night and a night or two of 7.5 hours. I like to use the paid version of the app called Sleep Cycle in my app store. The free one is good too, but I like the perks of the paid one. If you are someone who needs white noise or a noise machine, this app is great because it has that too! I choose the gentle wake up cycle they offer because I do not believe in shocking the body awake. I have no paid affiliation with them of any sort, I've tried other apps and this is my favorite.

If you slept the 8 hours we have heard about you would move right past the 7.5 hour mark and back into deep sleep waves. Then, if your alarm were to go off at this point you would wake feeling groggy and tired because you were smack in the middle of the cycle, as opposed to waking at 7.5 and feeling naturally alert. These time recommendations are not exact, so waking 5-10 mins before 6 hours or 7.5 is no big deal, ok? Give it a try and maybe even document how you felt that day to see how it differs from usual.

Most people have a bed time routine: wash the face, brush the teeth like a responsible adult etc. A beneficial one can be making sure that the temperature of your body and the room is cool. A hot body will not go to sleep quickly. If you like, take a hot bath before bed. The quick drop in body temperature after getting out of the water makes an ideal segue for bed. Some fine folks like to have a fan on in the room to keep it cool, or even a window open. These are great ways to keep a sleep conducive environment.

Practicing the breath exercise you learned above is great to get the body to prepped for Lala Land. So is learning Yoga Nidra, more breath work designed to calm the mind and body before sleep. A great website for this is 5809yoga. com There are 40, 51 and 17 minute ones to choose from. I like the 17 minute one, but explore! Meditation before bed is also fantastic, but do not meditate in your bed! You want your bed to be associated with sleeping, not meditation. Meditate on the floor next to bed or create a little space in your home where you can do these exercises. Prayer is also a great way to send the body off to sleep, especially prayers of gratitude. If prayer is your jam, go for it. Maybe even try mixing a few different things and find what works best for you.

Who doesn't have Coconut oil in their homes these days? If you don't, that's ok! You can find an oil for the body of your choice at your local health food store or even pharmacy. Take a little of this oil and rub it on the bottoms of your feet. Why? Reflexology shows us that rubbing the bottoms of our feet promotes relaxation of mind and body. Different areas on the bottom of the foot correspond to the organs in our bodies and the relaxation felt from this technique also prepares these systems for sleep. Please remember to be GENTLE to yourself while rubbing the feet. Pretend that you are rubbing the feet of a newborn baby and feel the sensations that come from this easy to do sleep aid.

Herbs and supplements are great for lulling the body into sleep too, however, it must be said that they be recommend for you by a licensed medical professional or practitioner. While I am a certified Ayurvedic Wellness Counselor, these are general recommendations. You are responsible for what you put in your body. Chamomile tea or sleepy time teas are another inexpensive and soothing way to calm the mind and body before sleep. In the late fall/winter and early spring I am a fan of Golden Milk, an Ayurvedic recipe that my whole family loves! It's like a delicious sleep promoting latte! The link to make this can be found at – https://www.youtube.com/watch?v=jYCQb2YNGt4&feature=youtu.be – Enjoy!

Once you are ready to hit the proverbial hay, make sure that hay is as comfortable as you can afford! We spend 1/3 of our lives sleeping and doing that as comfortably as possible is a recommended goal I share with everyone. I've spent on my bed and sheets as much as I'd spend on a family vacation. Every night is a vacation for our bodies from every way in which it served us throughout the day. Vacation well for yourself! Holidays like President's Day, Memorial and Labor Day weekends are a great time to invest in your sleep hygiene products like mattresses, sheets, pillows etc!

There you have it, folks! A few of the fine ways that I personally use to combat stress and fall asleep. I enjoy meditation and breath work practices and have built up to doing them for an hour a day. I'm a better version of me when I practice! You are ready to be your best you. Start slow. Be kind to yourself and be satisfied with your efforts. Lots of love from me to you.

Marisa is a Psychic/Medium, Energy healer and certified Ayurvedic Wellness Practitioner who is quite passionate about helping people find and sustain balance of mind, body, and spirit. Her expertise lies in advising clients on how to overcome the biggest concerns plaguing most: anxiety, sleep issues and stress management. She is an avid runner, yogi, wife and mother and would say her secret to success is that she is "heavily meditated"!

JEFFREY HANK

I CHING, COVID-19 & CURRENT EVENTS – A SHORT ESSAY

I just finished reading the complete "I Ching", with Confucian commentary, the ancient book of Chinese wisdom, parts of which are about 4,000 years old. This version of the I Ching clocks in at about 540 pages. While the prefaces about divination started out a little slow, initially causing me to put the book aside for a while, once I got back into it — it became a much more interesting read. Part religion, philosophy, art, literature, poetry, and history, it contains ethics and timeless wisdom about walking the Central Path, the Golden Mean, being truthful, upright, sincere, humble, and acting with Light, amongst other universal understandings of the ancient sages.

In a time where China is always in the news, it is interesting that such wisdom from so long ago remains so compelling, and I wonder how many Americans know much if anything about ancient Chinese culture. I wonder if the Chinese students in my town of East Lansing (Michigan State University is home to more Chinese students outside China than anywhere else in the world) encounter many Americans with an understanding or a curiosity. I wonder what they think of this microcosm of the 'West' and it's unique idiosyncrasies. Those Chinese students are learning our language and culture — how many of 'US' are learning 'theirs'? I wonder why growing up, even though receiving a good education, I didn't learn about Chinese history and civilization. In school you could sort of learn Spanish, or French, or maybe German, but not Mandarin or Arabic or Russian or Portuguese or Swahili. I wonder, if the Uighurs today in camps are losing their own culture and being indoctrinated with the modern propaganda of the CCP, rather than the teachings of Confucian knowledge,

Taoism, or other ancient wisdom that underlies so much of Chinese culture – and whether China's own guiding lights can cause it to correct course and offer the world it's spiritual wisdom rather than it's weapons or war.

I started this read pre-quarantine after reading the Bible and Quran cover-to-cover to switch up to some more 'Eastern' esoteric knowledge. I found some of the lessons universal. It is interesting how much of the wisdom of the I Ching and other ancient books of knowledge transcend cultures and times. Truth, Sincerity, but also Communication, dialogue, understanding, respect — these values and concepts are timeless amongst the sages, diplomats, and wise rulers and men and women of all learned cultures. There must be something to it....

Quarantine accelerated the accomplishment of finishing what is considered THE quintessential classic Chinese text. I think I will move onto reading another 'Eastern' revered book like the Mahabharata or something (open to suggestions for any ancient wisdom that is a must read from any culture to become more 'well-learned'). I have a friend who went to prison once and he read a lot of great books there, 250 in 2 years — more classics than most people ever get to in life. Carpe Diem. Bob Marley said, "Emancipate yourself from mental slavery. None but ourselves can free our mind." We're not in prison during quarantine, but if you're stuck at home not working as much and are going stir crazy, make good use of extra time if you can. It is more productive than arguing on facebook.

Perhaps off topic, but I worry about school kids around the globe missing instruction right now because they can't go in person, and internet learning is sub-par in most circumstances compared to individualized, in-person instruction. Poor American kids without internet are missing out short term, but even more egregious are the kids in Syria, Venezuela, and other conflict zones who are missing out even more. I'm fortunate enough to be able to mostly work from home although it is limiting and hurting business, and being productivity-oriented and a self-actualizing person fancying myself a renaissance man who will not 'rest on my laurels', I look at quarantine as almost a mandate to take more time to get more knowledge, and I'm reminded of the value of a good ol' fashion physical book – a book that can open doors of the mind and be shared with neighbors and passed down to future generations regardless if there is power, or internet, or viruses or storms, or an electronic book confiscation/censorship. It is probably time to re-open the libraries for the kids, sanctuaries and refuges for many people, and a place where knowledge is housed and diffused to people who seek it.

A book like the I Ching can bring perspective that is much needed at any time, and much appreciated in times of 'Change' — which is actually sort of what the I Ching is about – knowing that the only constant in life is Change. I hope that quarantine brings about reflection and change to everyone, change to politics, change to the economy, change to the environment, change to everyday life and how we treat each other and what we value as important. We all know about the negative health and economic consequences, now how do we make the best of a tough situation so the lessons are learned and things changed as positively as possible for the future? It is time for change individually and as a society – we should embrace it as opportunity and make the best of it. We have no other choice but to accept that change gon' come....

> *"Everything is in a continuous process of change. Change is absolute and certain; only the principle of change never changes."*
> – Between Heaven and Humanity, I Ching

I want to make it clear that nothing in this chapter should be considered anti-Chinese in any way, I have nothing but respect for Chinese people and culture and their accomplishments.

Is it not time for some positive change? Where are the leaders this generation desperately needs for this point in time? Read just a few of the headlines. Please come forward. The World needs you!

A Change is Gonna Come – Sam Cooke
https://www.youtube.com/watch?v=fPr3yvkHYsE

China Limited the Mekong's Flow. Other Countries Suffered a Drought
https://www.nytimes.com/2020/04/13/world/asia/china-mekong-drought.html?fbclid=IwAR36jJ8q9ti8l84MurVo8T4zM4NPFUUMlOsbmK2JSSs4Ip-mzSihJVJu6KSk

Brazil to Boost Amazon Forest Oversight as Deforestation Jumps
https://www.bloomberg.com/news/articles/2020-04-14/brazil-to-boost-ama-zon-forest-oversight-as-deforestation-jumps?fbclid=IwAR2NzFZHko_7stz-6mEDCzdEWmQ44dkYnPEOICGKPWODE6_UEAI5RvZnngHc

Detroit's poor air quality could be worsening the city's COVID-19 outbreak
https://www.fox2detroit.com/news/detroits-poor-air-quality-could-be-worsening-the-citys-covid-19-outbreak?fbclid=IwAR3Ffn6_X6--vJ3O4XYAkXkILD-r3oYU-oJ-QCZD9Zh7dUq5JKRNOURxSY54

Authoritarianism Vs. Democracy: How Will We Fight COVID-19?
https://therealnews.com/stories/authoritarianism-democracy-covid-19-coronavirus-harari-pandemic-liberalism-populism?fbclid=IwAR3oJ2eQFsavKLS6lVc-Biae74s5gW-PWpX1aDxI7l5QqvARS4hZpxgs4jaY

I'M READY FOR CHANGE. HOW ABOUT YOU?

Jeffrey Hank resides in East Lansing, Michigan. He is an attorney, entrepreneur, and political activist. He is married and enjoys family, traveling, reading, nature, and outdoor activities.

DR. JEAN LACOUR

RECOVERY WISDOM IN A SEASON OF CRISES

During the current global Coronavirus pandemic, many of us are experiencing a roller coaster of emotions, frustrating limitations and reactive thinking. If you are a person in recovery from substance misuse or from an addictive behavior like gambling or overeating, you may be feeling vulnerable and off balance with all the uncertainty and media melodrama.

I am here to call out to YOU to pause.... and remember. From your own personal addiction crises you discovered a life beyond anything you could hope for. You discovered a depth of meaning birthed during very painful circumstances. Remember your recovery tribe who invited you in, a loved one who waited in the background, perhaps your own spiritual awakening and Higher Power. Facing Addiction takes humility and courage. Please acknowledge your own experience, your strength and hope, your courage and service.

As we pause and step back, we can see that people around the world are experiencing the Coronavirus pandemic in ways that are similar to the destruction and chaos of addiction that impact families, companies, communities and nations.

We can recognize the same patterns of denial, anger (blaming), bargaining, depression, and finally, acceptance in the face of unexpected loss and pain. Yet we know that from acceptance arises deep gratitude and service. It is the same with this pandemic.

Just like a pebble tossed into a pond causes ripples of energy, I believe the larger recovery community has much to share in this season... a kindness, a word, a smile for people close to us. And a quiet confidence that life will offer new insight and a new normal with its own gifts.

Let's remember how large our recovery tribe is globally. Did you know there are over 24 million people just in the US who self-identify as being in recovery? Plus millions more worldwide who choose to remain private about their recovery.

For each person in recovery, there can be one or two loved ones who experienced the Miracle of Recovery for themselves.

If we include the people who reached out to help us, our ripple effect increases. Remember the people who helped make your healthy recovery possible… Counselors, therapists, recovery peers, Sponsors, Faith Leaders and professional recovery coaches who shared their wisdom.

As your gratitude expands, remember the Wisdom you have gained in the form of recovery practices and relationships in this season of crises.

1. **Speak Truth:** This Too Shall Pass; Easy Does It; Living One Day at a Time; "I didn't cause it, I can't cure it, and I can't control it"; Let Go and Let God; First Things First.
2. **Find Support Online:** try "In the Rooms" or SHE RECOV-ERS Together Online Facebook Group, or more resources at – https://netinstitute.org/aaft-resources/
3. **Take Action:** use a journal to date / capture your thoughts and feelings; remember self-care, eat, sleep (and enjoy it); interrupt compulsive cycles like overeating, oversharing or binge-watching movies, etc.

May you value the wisdom of your own recovery journey.

ONE THING I'VE LEARNED…

Imagine you could go back in time and share with your younger self **ONE THING** you've learned in your Recovery Journey that has been a real **aha!** revelation. What would that be for you? I recently asked this question to a special group of Professional Coaches who specialize in Addiction Recovery. Their answers were deep and thoughtful and worthy of sharing with you. I hope something will resonate with you.

Let these heart-spoken words flow from many hearts to yours. Each thought below begins with, "In my Recovery I discovered that… "

- I could, in fact, live without drugs and alcohol as part of my life. It is possible for me to live a life that is Happy, Joyous, and Free! The work is worth it! Never give up.
- That I wasn't just a 'bad kid' like my family labeled me. I was a child in

tremendous pain that didn't want to live. Being indigenous, it was life changing to learn about intergenerational trauma.

- The facts behind the neuroscience of addiction, and that even after years of drinking, I could indeed 're-wire' my brain.
- Learning the co-dependent roles in the drama triangle and how often I act in one of those roles with others!
- That alcohol is truly a poison. I know it sounds silly, but I honestly thought it was part of a healthy lifestyle. I had no idea how much it affected my brain, hormones, etc. My drinking went from normal to not normal very quickly after my children were born.
- I am not alone, there is a way out, that's when things got so much better.
- I wish I would have known how difficult the transition from a program to being on my own was going to be. It can be lonely learning to be honest, humble, and authentic.
- That I had a relationship with (booze, money, sex, food) driven by beliefs, and physical needs, and that the relationship COULD change.
- I was so trapped in the shame cycle: drink, behave badly, feel guilt and shame, drink to feel differently. I wish I had known more about the disease of alcoholism and how it affected my brain chemistry.
- That I wasn't in control of anyone except myself. This seems simple but it took the focus off my own addiction and kept me in denial while I was "helping" everyone else. Letting go of that and harnessing the power to propel my own life forward has opened so many new doors!
- That there are many pathways to recovery. There was one particular path that worked for me and the people I loved but it might not work for everyone.
- I wished I'd known about the link between addiction and trauma and that what I experienced during childhood really was trauma. It's been quite a journey for sure, but totally worth it!
- My thoughts and emotions do not have to ruin my life.

Take time to consider a few of your own **aha!** recovery revelations. You will be glad you did.

TAMING OUR WILD EMOTIONS

Along my own recovery journey, it seemed that most people I met felt one of three strong emotions: mad, sad or afraid, or some negative variation! Someone has said that Emotion is "Energy in Motion." I remember using the energy of anger or fear regularly to propel me into action – usually a thoughtless reaction to someone or something!

Have you ever wanted to hit an invisible pause button to calm yourself down when you're feeling upset, angry or frustrated? Well, there's good news from brain science and from research on Emotional Intelligence about ways we can learn to tame our emotions and reduce our stress in the moment.

Last fall I found myself slowing to a standstill on an Interstate highway…not a good sign when I was running late and have a deadline. As far as I could see, traffic was barely moving but a man was trying to cut in front of me. I focused my full irritation on him. *HE* was my problem…which was totally irrational.

Then I recalled what I was learning about Emotional Intelligence. I said to myself, "It's not his fault. I'm really frustrated sitting here with no good alternatives." Strangely, I felt better. I relaxed my shoulders, checked my mobile phone, and turned on the radio. I was still stuck in my car but with less tension. The simple act of **recognizing** my frustration seemed to help reduce its intensity. Instead of fuming or blaming, I just acknowledged it and named it.

According to Joshua Freedman, a pioneer in the science of Emotional Intelligence (EQ), naming emotions seems to bridge the gap between thoughts and feelings. He explains that the step from "I am this…" to "I am feeling this…." or even "Jean is feeling this….", means that we are NOT that emotion. It can remind us that an emotion is temporary.

No matter where we are in our recovery, we can be 'blindsided' by strong emotions including the emotional 'flatness' of depression. Learning a simple tool to help diminish the raw intensity of our emotions can build our hopefulness and our confidence.

Naming one's emotions is a simple but liberating experience. Someone said it's like coming to a stop sign at a busy intersection. It gives you a moment to pause and check in with yourself. Naming the feeling in the moment can bring a sense of calm as it defuses your focus on the "problem" and brings your attention and awareness back inside.

I invite you to experiment and see if it helps. Becoming aware of what you're feeling is the first step to increasing your Emotional Intelligence. I am feeling optimistic about you and your recovery. So, let's stay together. Read on for more tips and tools.

TURNING DOWN OUR INNER NOISE

In the midst of the Coronavirus pandemic, we can become stressed by all "the noise" coming from the talking heads and conflicting news flooding the airways about COVID-19 (Coronavirus). The media stirs up intense negativity through accusations, blaming and infighting at a time when all of us need to find common ground and take care for ourselves and others.

Tens of thousands of people have been sent home to work remotely without their team, work structure or accountability; many people must now 'homeschool' their children while maintaining their work output through Microsoft Teams, Slack, Zoom or Skype, etc.

Consider this, millions of people who are in recovery or dealing with mental health issues, along with tens of thousands of older adults are expected to go into isolation for weeks on end without the social support and activities that have sustained them. Financial uncertainty along with "social distancing" increases stress levels.

Fact: Many people will turn to alcohol, substances and other addictive behaviors to 1) cope with negative stress 2) deal with the monotony and dullness of being cut off from social contact.

Fact: We have choices; we have practices, skills and tools. I've created a few reminders to support us in healthy ways.

The word **B-A-I-T** is my short list of mood states that can lead to relapse.

B – Boring: be aware of **Boredom** that can drain your resources and creativity

A – Anxious…Angry: every negative statistic seems designed to make us fret with **Anxiety**. We become **Angry** about feeling out of control of our finances or the risks of getting sick.

I – Isolated… being **Alone** at home away from our workplace or support groups or friends wears us down. Being **isolated** with our own thoughts and the voices in our head makes the situation worse.

T – Triggered… to experience an emotional reaction to something based out of your previous history… people, places, things, smells, music, etc. Triggers put us into a mental / emotional place of distress and feeling out of control.

The **BAIT** words represent the states of emotion we experience as a *recurring thought or voice in our heads*, such as: "I can't take this, don't know what I'm going to do, what if I get sick, etc."

These inner thoughts might tell us to "use… just a little" to get some relief. This is when we must choose to turn down the inner noise and step back.

But how do we do this? Start with a **piece of P-I-E…**

P – Pause: push pause on your thoughts and feelings. Notice what is really in the present. Do you have food, clothes, a place to sleep, cash, a friend or sponsor to call, or access to the internet to reconnect with people?

I – Inhale: you can quickly neutralize your anxious intensity and actually switch your nervous system from "fight or flight" (sympathetic nervous system) to "rest and digest" (parasympathetic nervous system). Try it. Take a deep breath! Hold it a bit and slowly exhale… do this again paying attention to the sound of your breath.

You will reduce your feelings of anxiety, anger, isolation, or whatever triggers you to feel out of control. Do whatever brings you back to the present moment. Stretch, wiggle your toes, put on music, splash water on your face… notice what is around you. Continue to take deep breaths and help your body to release its intensity.

E – Express: grab a notebook and start writing as quickly as you can. Let your inner thoughts and feelings flow across the pages. Express your thoughts in a way that does not bring harm to you or others. Call a friend or sponsor or caring family member who encourages you. Express your feelings to your Higher Power, to the God of your understanding. Express your gratitude as you look around you. Be thankful for your coffee or tea, for warm clothes, for your sobriety.

You will discover that **PIE** (Pause, Inhale, Express) along with a cup of gratitude, will release a flood of 'feel good' neurotransmitters and increase your sense of calm and wellbeing in the midst of any challenge.

Remember, you are incredibly valuable - to yourself and to all of us. Check out our Recovery Resources and pass them on. And please, listen for the applause, it's all around you.

Dr. LaCour is a global consultant who equips Addiction-Concerned leaders, businesses, professionals, and individuals to prevent and reduce the impact of addiction through non-clinical online Certification programs. She is founder/CEO of NET Institute Center for Addiction and Recovery Education that has served 40,000 students in over 35 nations.
https://www.linkedin.com/in/jeanlacour/

ENCOURAGED THROUGH CHRIST

I am writing this chapter from my home in Mozambique, Africa. We are on lockdown and I have 4 visitors from 3 different countries that cannot go home at the moment. We understand how others are feeling. After 25 years on the Mission Field in South Africa and Mozambique, I know, even people who do not usually attend church or listen to preachers, will listen to missionaries testify about the miracles they have seen personally or our endless stories about seeing God move in 3rd world countries.

Besides stories about our cross cultural experiences, language learning and cultural mishaps we are often asked how we cope with seeing so much suffering in the world? They ask,"How do you not get hardened? Are you afraid of anything?"

I think living in adverse conditions for years can be very challenging, but it can also be very rewarding. Most of the rewards we only realize we have gained in times like these. I am thinking of several missionary families that I know who were called back to their home countries, this past week, so that they could be together with their older children who are in University. Their hearts were torn, between returning for their adult children and leaving those they love here, as well as, being exposed to more "danger en route." Thank God they all arrived safely.

I was thinking today about how everyone of us missionaries has been through life threatening bouts of sickness; some have been through wars, tsunamis, riots, coups, earthquakes, and armed robberies. Some have buried loved ones on the mission field, some have even been imprisoned for their faith. All have been threatened more than once in their years of service to the Lord on the mission field, in various ways. All of us have had to trust our lives and the lives of those we love to the Lord on a daily basis, as do all of you living in this world. I think for the most part working in third world countries exposes us to life and death issues or struggles daily, in a way that maybe only healthcare professionals deal with in the First World.

As for me and my house we will serve the Lord.

My life is hidden with Christ, in God. I gave my life away a long time ago that I may find a new life in Christ. I am not preaching to you, I am testifying – there is a difference. My hope in writing this short chapter to encourage people through these trying times is that you will be encouraged, exhorted to focus and change what needs changing, and that you would remember what you already know...or may have been told. My prayer is that you would be able to breathe deeply and relax as you read and refocus.

I am not worried, or afraid, I am not terrified or dismayed. I am confident that HE who started a good work in me will be faithful to complete it in His time and in His way. I only need to cooperate with Him and yield to His leadership, His Lordship in my life.

Oftentimes, we want the benefits of a close loving and committed relationship without putting in the effort. We want all the blessings without the obedience, the surrender "your will, not mine, be done here O Lord". I would encourage you as you have more "time" than usual to consider where you are at in your spiritual life. How much peace do you have or where do you find it, if you have lost it? So many people call a friend who has faith when they are doubting or fearful...why keep calling them when you can call on God yourself?

Much of what I have seen has been informative, some of what I have heard on FB or other social media channels however is either very negative, cultivating fear and or mocking - flat out blaspheming the Holy Spirit. I think these are some of the very things God wants to address during our worldwide "timeout."

As Christ Followers, we believe we have a huge opportunity to see reconciliation and healing of the family unit globally. We trust God is working all of this out for our good. Yes, lives have been lost and people have suffered, it is tragic and sad. I do not deny that and there is a place, "to weep with those who weep," and our hearts go out to all suffering loss or sickness at this time. We need to pray for the world, for countries we rarely think of, for people we do not know and for our neighbors right next door. Truth is we are more connected than we know. Funny how every nationality has had the same symptoms, all of us are human.

I hope in spending time in the same space with your loved ones that you remember what made you fall in love with that "hunk" of a man sitting across the table from you, or what you love about each of your unique children. I hope you laugh so hard you cry at your sister or brothers corny jokes. I hope you play cards and board games, that you do puzzles and play Pictionary or Apples to Apples. I hope you feel like you are at summer camp with your kids and that you guys make memories and music and refocus on the things that matter… each other. I hope that we put our phones down and do some real face to face fellowshipping and enjoy Skype or Zoom calls with our family members far away. I see so many people have become creative, playing games and interacting with their elderly loved ones via the internet. That is great!!!

I know churches have made their sermons or worship sessions available online. Maybe this has been a way to get more churches "up to speed with technology". God will use all things for our good. It is not just megachurches that have good messages, encouraging small groups or Bible Studies. We all have something to offer.

Two scripture verses have been on my mind all day; "As for me and my house, we will serve the Lord." And the other verse; "my life is hidden with Christ in God."

People always ask me why I have stayed so long on the mission field, when things have been so challenging or there is so much heartache in the world.

My answer is that I was called to Mozambique when I was 12 and that I believe I was born to do this. I believe I must also live my purpose not just help others find theirs and live it. They always ask, "Aren't you afraid of malaria, or traffickers or other dangers?" My answer is "no, I am not afraid. I am not afraid to live my purpose, to obey God and follow Him into places, to get people that He loves and longs to restore. I am not afraid, not because I am "stupid" or "unaware of the risks" but because I know my life has value, I know Jesus died for me and that in doing that He gave me new life, eternal life. Whatever happens to me or however I transition to eternity is not my focus. My focus is living a life worthy of His sacrifice and Him dying for me. I just want to thank Him and in doing so I want to live in a manner worthy. The fact is because of my decision to accept Jesus Christ as my Saviour, my life is now hidden with Christ in God. Even if I die physically, I will not die spiritually. I believe I will just transition to heaven and get a new body and spend eternity with God.

Some of you may have heard a hard core missionary or a Hells angels biker say something like that and you wondered, *what the heck does that mean?*.. more than sounding hard core, it is true. I am not afraid, I died a long time ago, meaning in accepting Jesus free gift of salvation. I exchanged my old sinful life for a new life in Christ where I have the Holy Spirit to lead and guide me to teach me all I need to know about Jesus and my Heavenly Father and I have everything I need for life and Godliness. It means I do not have to carry the weight of my sin, guilt, shame or grief, I can exchange all of that mess for all HE offers. All it takes is my bowing my knee, acknowledging that I need a savior. I must confess that I need Him and HE is more than willing to come to my rescue and deliver me from myself.

So many people are offended by the simplicity of the Gospel. I personally want to encourage you with a few simple things that may help you focus and keep perspective in these trying times:

1. The Bible says cast your burdens unto Jesus for He cares for you.
2. Pour your complaints before the Lord. It is ok to tell Him you are afraid, or angry, sad or discouraged. HE can handle it HE will not condemn you for being honest. He will console you and give you peace in exchange for anxiety, hope for despair. He can heal your physical body, protect you from sickness and deliver you safely to the other side of this pandemic, whole, healed and full of joy in life despite the crazy time you just passed through. He did not promise these things would not happen, he actually said He would be with us through these times. Trust Him.
3. Value life. Some of us have become desensitized to the value of the people around us. We have become rude, inconsiderate, pushy, bossy, selfish -in some cases bullies. "Get out of my way!" "my way" was to ask God what His way would be for the day HE has given me?."
4. Part of this, is that we now get to feel what others have felt for years: there is a lack of hospitals, quality technology and care facilities, resources and workers.
5. We have said in Africa for years, *"remember there is something likeable, special, worth celebrating in all of us."*
6. Worship not because He makes you feel good, or it makes you look good, but because He is worthy. It is really all about Him anyway.

For those of you struggling during this time, please be encouraged to know you are not alone. People around the world that you do not even know are praying for you right now. They are crying out to God for your protection, for mercy and grace, for your healing and for peace to be poured over you and your families. There are more people praying globally about this subject than any other, at the moment. As I said, we feel for those infected now and are praying for them and their families. We do not lose hope and will, we continue praying.

When things get difficult or you feel overwhelmed. Look for a way to be a blessing to someone else. Look for a creative way to make someone's day. This can still be done while self-isolating or while others are in quarantine or lockdown.

Draw a picture, record a message or a song, send someone a song that made you happy or spoke to your heart. Write an email letter or card telling those people you miss the things you appreciate about them. Those words are powerful and precious. I can guarantee you long after we are through this ordeal those words will still matter to whoever received them. They may even hang on someone's wall.

In December 2001, Ms. Katie Magill *fulfilled a lifelong calling and established herself as a Christian missionary in Mozambique, Africa. The vision of Ms. Magill's ministry was to redeem the purpose of women and children whose lives had been targeted by sex traffickers. For nearly fifteen (15) years Katie Magill's ministry, known as Project Purpose, has worked alongside governmental agencies reaching out to trafficked women and children.*

ROB CRISELL

THE OUTSTRETCHED HAND & OTHER CONSOLATIONS OF POETRY

I

In 1821, the poet John Keats—self-quarantined with a dear friend who served as his nurse—lay dying of tuberculosis, coughing up blood in a small house at the foot of the Spanish Steps. He was 25 years old. Toward the end, Keats would sometimes cry upon waking, to find himself still alive. The following fragment of poetry was found among his papers:

> "This living hand, now warm and capable
> Of earnest grasping, would, if it were cold
> And in the icy silence of the tomb,
> So haunt thy days and chill thy dreaming nights
> That thou would wish thine own heart dry of blood
> So in my veins red life might stream again,
> And thou be conscience-calm'd—see here it is—
> I hold it towards you."

Like much great verse, this little poem is incurably ambiguous. However, many readers, including myself, think that Keats—misunderstood, abused, and miserable for much of his life—is addressing future readers like us, stretching out his hand to those who would grasp it. His dream is that we might be "conscience-calm'd," which I take to mean "heartened" or "consoled." At the same time, he imagines that if we grasp his hand, we once again would see "red life" flow through his veins. He's receiving and giving blood. He's a friend. The poem is a powerful image of the mysterious commerce that exists between poets and readers, through time and space, across languages and cultures.

Throughout my life, I have often turned to poetry for clarity and consolation, especially during stressful and uncertain times. In light of recent events, it won't surprise you that I've been reading and writing a lot of poetry lately. In this essay, I will try to explain why I find poems so useful. Along the way, I will introduce you to some old friends that have helped me over the years. Maybe they can help you, too.

II

Besides being a writer and an actor, I teach Shakespeare and poetry to students in a medium-sized city in Southern California. In fact, the day before the state of California ordered all public schools closed due to the outbreak, I was explaining to six different fifth-grade classes how and why they should read poetry. Most of the hundreds of children to whom I've introduced Shakespeare and poetry have discovered something useful and profound in a certain poem and in themselves. Poetry's most valuable lessons have little to do with meter, rhyme, alliteration, metaphor, and so on. Great poems have less to do with a poet's skill, and more with connections the poet makes between herself, her readers, and the divine.

If that hasn't been your experience with poetry, you're not alone. Poetry is a dead art for most people. (Though I would argue that there's little difference between well-written songs and well-written poems, but we'll leave that aside for now.) Poems are about as relevant to our lives as macramé or the proper conjugation of Latin verbs.

Poet and scholar Dana Gioia explains this phenomenon in his seminal essay *Can Poetry Matter?*:

> "American poetry…has become the specialized occupation of a relatively small and isolated group. Like priests in a town of agnostics, poets still command a certain residual prestige. But as individual artists they are almost invisible."

Or as American poet Marianne Moore famously put it in the first line of her poem entitled (duh!) *Poetry*: "I too, dislike it." Poems, she writes, are "useful" only if they can create "imaginary gardens with real toads in them."

Imaginary gardens with real toads in them.

Perhaps that line gives you a spasm of confusion, dread, even frustration. I certainly had that sensation when I read it for the first time. I hear you say: "Curse you, poetry! There you go again." Or it just makes you feel ignorant— vaguely aware of your unawareness. Well, join the club. As I tell my students, the best poetry makes you sweat a little. For me, Moore's line has something to do with how the best poems can take us from the *visible* to the *invisible*. In Owen Barfield's words, poetry marks the "forgotten relations" between things and among people. It bridges the chasm.

In my opinion, dead poets are best at this kind of bridging. They're done with all the strife of existence. They've lived through wars, plagues, riots, and revolutions. They're finished with "joy and moan," as Shakespeare's writes. As Henry Longfellow memorably puts in *A Psalm to Life*:

> Lives of great men all remind us
> We can make our lives sublime,
> And, departing, leave behind us
> Footprints on the sands of time;
>
> Footprints, that perhaps another,
> Sailing o'er life's solemn main,
> A forlorn and shipwrecked brother,
> Seeing, shall take heart again.

Poets tell us to take heart. They remind us that we have a friend who knows exactly what we're going through. Maybe that friend wants to make us laugh, like Lear, Nash, Dahl, and Silverstein. Maybe they want to tell us a story, like Dante, Shakespeare, Milton, and Poe. Maybe they want to break our heart, like Sophocles, Yeats, Sassoon, Plath, and Bishop. Whatever it is a poet does, he or she is there to remind us—in a new way—what it is like to be a human being.

Reading and writing poetry is a way of *thinking*. A well-known definition of a poem is where "a feeling has found its thought, and a thought has found its words." Poetry evokes emotion, and that emotion evokes thought—and often transformation. Poems are at their most powerful when they resound with a feeling that we have within us. They alert us to what is deepest in ourselves.

Here are few other poetic descriptions of a poem, which can be found in Edward Hirsch's outstanding book *How to Read a Poem and Fall in Love with Poetry*:

- A message in a bottle;

- A soul in action through words;
- A speaking picture;
- The bloodiest of art forms;
- Language compressed and raised to its highest power;
- A time bomb designed to explode on contact.

If none of these metaphors resonates with you, that's all right. Poetry is one way of thinking, but it's certainly not a popular way these days. In our modern world—especially with the surreal overlay of the coronavirus—our language is increasingly literal and prosaic. Today, for example, our dialogue is dominated by dreary words like epidemiology, germs, health care, containment, PPE, viruses, contagion, isolation, social distancing, lockdown, etc. We retreat to the safety of our various tribes. We look for existential meaning in science and politics, blaming or championing ideologies or leaders. We even dull our minds with food, alcohol, drugs, mindless entertainment, and other distractions.

All of this is normal and understandable. But as Hamlet—that sublime philosopher-poet and everyman—puts it:

> "W h a t   i s   a   m a n ,
> If   his   chief   good   and   market   of   his   time
> Be but to sleep and feed? a beast, no more."

Even a beast washes itself and avoids infection if it can. Even beasts seek protection with friends and kinfolk. Only humans search for meaning outside the physical plane. Only humans are poets, philosophers, and artists.

III

After governments around the world shut down much of civilization and banished all to our collective rooms, I instinctively turned to poetry (also faith, family, friends, music, the arts—I'm not crazy!) to help me navigate the sadness, fear, and chaos:

- First, a theater director and friend began a series of "Quarantine Monologues" from William Shakespeare as a way to reach out to the arts community. I was the first to contribute a speech (or two).
- Second, I completed yet another draft of my verse adaptation of Sophocles' *Electra* for a theater company that is producing it in the fall.

- Third, I began a daily feature on my <u>Facebook page</u> and <u>YouTube Channel</u> I call it, "30 Poems of Hope and Joy in 30 Days." Every day, I select and recite a well-known poem, sharing a few observations as well as a biography of the poet.
- Fourth, I submitted a Shakespearean sonnet recitation (mine was Sonnet 32) as part of an <u>online sonnet series</u> in which 154 actors from all over the world perform all 154 of Shakespeare's sonnets. I acted in a <u>live dramatic online reading</u> of *Much Ado About Nothing* and *Merry wives of Windsor* with an all-star cast of actors (myself notwithstanding). Later this month, I also took part in a dramatic reading of *King Lear*.
- Fifth, I put a case of wine under a fake boulder at the top of my driveway and invited various friends to give me their favorite poem in exchange for a bottle of wine. I received poems by Gabriel Garcia Lorca, Plath, Poe, MacLeish, Millay, James Thomson, as well as a couple originals.
- Sixth, I recorded <u>several videos</u> that teachers have asked me to create to help their students with poetry and Shakespeare. I'm currently creating an entire online poetry course for a local middle school.
- Finally, I wrote—and continue to write—poems, including several poking fun at the <u>virus</u> (they were funnier a few weeks ago). I wrote nine haikus about my <u>chickens</u>. My favorite poem so far is one I wrote about <u>frogs</u>. I'm currently working on a poem tentatively entitled "Put a Penny on the Plague Stone." Don't ask.

Thanks to all this activity, I have a stronger mental and spiritual foundation that I hope will help me weather the thousand natural shocks that will visit us over the next weeks and months. I have "shored these fragments against my ruins," in the words of T.S. Eliot. I hope these fragments, however, help you, too. I've tried to provide certain poetic and artistic resources for others, while also helping myself. Trust me—everyone benefits from a wiser, happier, less anxious me.

Before you go, allow me to introduce you to a few dozen old friends with whom I've been reacquainting myself during the quarantine. See? Here they are—they hold out their hands to you…

– Rob Crisell April 2020

- <u>THIS LIVING HAND</u> – John Keats
- <u>A PSALM OF LIFE</u> – Henry Wadsworth Longfellow
- <u>NO MAN IS AN ISLAND</u> – John Donne
- <u>JABBERWOCKY</u> – Lewis Carroll

- "HOPE" IS THE THING WITH FEATHERS – Emily Dickinson
- THE LAKE ISLE OF INNISFREE – William Butler Yeats
- DO NOT GO GENTLE INTO THAT GOOD NIGHT – Dylan Thomas
- SONNET 29 – William Shakespeare
- GOD'S GRANDEUR – Gerard Manley Hopkins
- MORNING SONG – Sylvia Plath
- EXCERPT FROM THE FOUR ZOAS – William Blake
- HOW DO I LOVE THEE? – By Elizabeth Barrett Browning
- SEA FEVER – John Masefield
- A BOY NAMED SUE – Shel Silverstein
- THERE WILL COME SOFT RAINS – Sara Teasdale
- THE DYING CHRISTIAN TO HIS SOUL – Alexander Pope
- THE BOXER – Paul Simon
- POETRY - Marianne Moore
- TRAVEL – Edna St. Vincent Millay
- THE WASTELAND – T.S. Eliot
- THE WORLD IS TOO MUCH WITH US – William Wordsworth
- MACAVITY: THE MYSTERY CAT – T.S. Eliot
- INVICTUS – William Ernest Henley
- STOPPING BY THE WOODS ON A SNOWY EVENING – Robert Frost
- THOSE WINTER SUNDAYS – Robert Hayden
- IF – Rudyard Kipling
- NO COWARD SOUL IS MINE – Emily Brontë
- SHE WALKS IN BEAUTY – Lord Byron
- THE SECOND COMING – William Butler Yeats
- THE DREAM OF THE ROOD – Anonymous (8th century AD)
- PRAYER – Dana Gioia
- CAN POETRY MATTER? – (from *The Atlantic*) By Dana Gioia
- HOW TO READ A POEM AND FALL IN LOVE WITH POETRY – Edward Hirsch

Rob Crisell is a writer, actor, educator, and attorney in Southern California. After two decades in publishing, national non-profit work, law, and commercial real estate, he's now is a full-time writer. For details check out his website at robcrisell.com or subscribe to youtube.

10XING FAMILY, BUSINESS, & BABIES DURING CORONAVIRUS

Accountable Equity, Capital Group & Investor Mastermind leaders Melanie & Josh McCallen share how they 10X "ed" their life during Coronavirus.

Dear Readers, we are honored to be included in this powerful project by the "Last Life Ever" community. We love what Last Life Ever is doing for all of us as we seek to grow during the Coronavirus, and we hope this new book will herald in the launch of the "Last Life Ever Publishing Division."

In Ryan Holliday's NYT Best Selling book, "The Obstacle is the Way", he shared that growth is only possible when we overcome obstacles. In a sense, the "Obstacle" is the way to growth. Melanie and I are passionate about loving the people in our lives during this Covid-19 Pandemic. We hope our story-dialogue below, which we transcribed during a Capital Hacking podcast episode will empower you to 10X your growth because of (not in-spite of) Covid-19. The best way to beat a pandemic is to turn this negative situation into the greatest source of power for personal growth that you and I may ever have in our lifetime.

Just a quick disclaimer: We know that our 10 child family is a "bit of an outlier" for today's world, so, we hope that the 10X mentality of our family size doesn't overshadow how each of us readers can benefit from this Real-World case study of how one family and business used the Coronavirus for good.

So, without further ado (the most over used cliché in podcasting) let's get to the story...

We are honored to share a live transcription from the popular Capital Hacking podcast with all of the wonderful people of Last Life Ever:

Josh McCallen: This is the at-home Capital Hacking edition with the illustrious Melanie McCallen

Erik Cabral: Melanie, how are you? The audience and the tribe wants to know how you're feeling.

Melanie McCallen: Well, I'm here with one of my kids, with my youngest child, my sweet little boy, three weeks old.

Erik Cabral: We know and love the McCallens. We want to hear how they're dealing with life, real life during the Coronavirus pandemic.

How are you guys fairing? I mean, you are one of the few, if not the only families I know that had a child during this craze. Tell us how it all happened.

Melanie McCallen: Well, gosh, this whole Coronavirus thing! I think it came quick for all of us, right? I can remember - being nine months pregnant, ready to go anytime - and hearing there was one case in Washington state. And I thought, *Well, okay, one case, too bad it ended up here in America, but here we go.* And all of a sudden within a week, all my kids were home from school, and everything was shutting down. And so, it was pretty clear I was going to be having a baby at a VERY interesting time.

Josh McCallen: Time out; Melanie is nursing Baby Coyle, he's just such a microphone hog. It's ridiculous. Erik this guy is always getting on camera. Babies these days Erik they're born with an Instagram account, I swear.

Melanie McCallen: Following in his Dad's footsteps.

Erik Cabral: I think we're making podcast history. The youngest Capital Hacking guest on the show, three weeks old, born just a few weeks ago.

Josh McCallen: Aw, Mr. Coyle

Melanie McCallen: That's right. So anyhow I went to the hospital for a checkup, about a week before the baby, or no, just days actually. It was bizarre because the hospital was on lockdown and there were very few cars. You had to go through these cement barricades. I was a military kid, so it reminded me of a military lockdown. At the air force base, they would do these routine drills with these cement barricades, with people standing there asking you questions. And I'm like, wow, this is really something.

Then they decided this baby was never going to come out and he was going to end up being about 11 or 12 pounds if I didn't deliver soon. So we decided to do an induction and they were describing this process of entering the Labor and Delivery ward, "You'll need to go around the back and they'll escort you through –" and all this sort of stuff.

It was bizarre and very different than any other baby I've had, that's for sure. It was also my first induction, so that was kind of history making too. But everything went well, Josh was able to be with me, thank goodness. I was getting a little nervous about that since they were only allowing one person in the hospital with you. And, they had you answer a series of questions. "Have you been on a cruise ship? Have you been near anybody on a cruise ship? And Josh almost was, but he wasn't.

Josh McCallen: Yeah so, many crazy coincidences. Melanie and I often work at the Renault Resort itself (Melanie focuses on design). Well, the Vivâmee Hospitality Vice President, Dan Alicea, had been on a cruise ship when the Coronavirus broke out. And he had been back to work for about five days or so before the baby came. Miraculously, we had so much going on during that period we never went to the resort to work.

Melanie McCallen: Dan Alicea is a great guy. He's awesome. And thank God nobody got sick on his cruise ship. They were all able to come home…

Josh McCallen: Good old Dan Alicea, We love that guy and I almost went to work with him but luckily I didn't…

Melanie McCallen: And I remember waking up one morning and having this epiphany. I said, "Josh what if they ask us if you've been near anybody on a cruise?" And sure enough, that's the second question they asked when we pulled up! I looked right at Josh and I said, what if you had to say yes, would I be delivering this baby by myself?

Erik Cabral: Oh my Goodness!

Josh McCallen: But we're grateful it worked out well while we were there. Of course, exact outcomes depend on what happens during the actual birthing process. And, Melanie was able to have a natural birth with the induction. So, thank God no C-section. That's always a blessing. And what number baby is this, Melanie?

Melanie McCallen: You need me to remind you??

Josh McCallen: That was a question for the audience. It just happens that I asked it. Erik you should have asked that. Melanie's right.

Erik Cabral: For anyone who doesn't know, they're in double digits.

Melanie McCallen: Coyle made ... number 10. And he also made the boys happy in the family because now we have our four boys and our six ladies. So, he was a big surprise.

Nobody knew if it was a boy or girl, so that was exciting. Josh McCallen: Yeah, we were excited.

Erik Cabral: Great news - during a chaotic time or what was gearing up to be a chaotic time. I'm curious, what was his birthday?

Melanie McCallen: March 18th

Josh McCallen: It was the day all those press conferences were called by the President and Andrew Cuomo. That's the day that it all started.

Erik Cabral: Wow.

Josh McCallen: Yea, his birthday was the day they were holding three-hour press conferences discussing getting the national guard and hospitals ready, and lockdowns underway; and you're like, what?

We were in the hospital and it was all starting. So, here's an inside scoop. We're obviously in the labor and delivery maternity ward. And the staff there was not as nervous. I will be honest with you, the doctors were like, "This is overblown, it's all going to be over quickly, don't worry about it." So, we got a sense that not everybody was on the same page. It turns out that everything got pretty serious after that.

Melanie McCallen: Honestly, after I delivered him, within minutes, they said, are you going to want to go home soon?

I said, "How long am I allowed to stay?"

I need a little buffer before I went home to the other nine you know, haha wink,wink. But seriously, our other kids were initially disappointed because no one was able to come visit the baby. But thank God for technology. We were all able to Facetime and they were able to be right there in the room with us.

And the kids were so sweet, when we came home, they had decorated the house and were just so excited. It was great coming home. And honestly, the baby's been a beautiful distraction during all of this.

The kids are hilarious. When I got home from the hospital, my three-year-old said something about Coronavirus. I was like, how does she even know that word? I guess it's so much in the background. And she doesn't know it's something to be nervous about. She just knows that's the reason she can't go visit her grandmother. We're just being careful. Cute little story, Josh's mom lives next door to us. So she's like, I can't go see Nana because of Coronavirus.

But, the other day she just went on her own. Our backyards connect, so she was able to just walk over. Normally she knocks on her back door and they go play puzzles or whatever.

It's very sweet. So, she knocked on Nana's door and said, Nana, can I come in? And Nana said no. My daughter said, "It's okay, Nana. Coronavirus is over." Later, Josh's Mom called to tell us the story. It was hilarious. She's such a funny little girl. She is very sweet.

Erik Cabral: It's funny, I think there's going to be the equivalent to, or something very similar to what happened after the second world war with baby boomers. I think there's going to be something I'm coining the Corona kids where it's like a boom in the population over these months, you know, three, four, five, nine months, however long it takes.

But I don't think Coyle will fall in that category.

Melanie McCallen: He was born right at the beginning of it. Josh McCallen: He'll be gypped of that special title

Erik Cabral: They might try to put him in that category, and he'll say, ah, I was made nine months before all that happened.

Melanie McCallen: The funny thing is I was excited about this baby being born in March. I remember finding out my due date and thinking, this is great, cold and flu season will be pretty much over. And here we are in a full pandemic.

Erik Cabral: Oh Goodness

The baby has a very unique name, and I'm sure the audience is curious as I am, the origins and how you guys came around to, to name him Coyle.

Melanie McCallen: Yeah. It's a unique name. We're all used to saying it, but it was kind of hard to mull it over in our heads for a little while how it was going to work. But the long and short of it is I have a very special grandmother who died about a year and a half ago – backbone of the family. You know, prayed for all of us by name all the time. She was such a faithful, strong, wonderful woman. We were all at the funeral up in New York. And, the day that she died, I was having some pain and I had just discovered I was pregnant a couple of days before and I was having a lot of severe pain on the day of her funeral.

We were planning on coming home with everybody after the funeral. It was a morning funeral. But I started feeling too sick to do that. So I ended up going to the emergency room right there in that area and found out I had an ectopic pregnancy. I had to have emergency surgery because I was already bleeding.

They basically told me if I had gotten in the car and driven home, I probably would have died in the car. It would have been a severe rupture. That happened on the day of her funeral. And a year later, right on the day that she died -the anniversary of the date that she died- I found out that I was pregnant with Coyle.

And I've felt really strongly all along that she's rooting for us; that this baby was a blessing from her. And, you know, she's the one we called whenever any of us -my siblings- were in labor. We always called up grandma and asked her to start praying because her prayers are so powerful.

So I like to say she's sort of the patron Saint of laboring mothers and anybody can pray to her if they want to: Sheila Coyle is her maiden name. So that's where we got the name Coyle.

Josh McCallen: Yeah Melanie's been asking for that name since we found out we were pregnant. She was pregnant with Coyle and that name's been hard for me to accept. I really didn't want that name. Mr. Coyle. I'm sorry buddy.

However, after a while it grew on me. And I said let's do it, Melanie, whatever you want. He was born the day after St Patrick's day, so a nice, strong Irish name kind of made sense right around then. Yeah. He almost was born on St Patrick's day.

There's no reason he couldn't have been born that day except, of course, they arranged his induction. That's right. They arranged his induction the next day, but he was already ready to be born. That guy was fully cooked.

Melanie McCallen: He was nine pounds 12 ounces. He was a monster.

Erik Cabral: Yeah. Unreal. He's super long too, right? I mean, he's not only practically 10 pounds, but what was his length?

Melanie McCallen: 21 and a half inches or so, I think.

Josh McCallen: Yeah, it happened during a really, absolutely unparalleled and crazy time. So I'm just glad everyone's happy and healthy, and you guys got through it. I mean, there was a lot happening in the business as well.

There was a mastermind at Renault. There were all these meetings, all these brides, all these people coming through. Talk a little bit about what that was like, getting ready to give birth with so much happening at once.

Melanie McCallen: Little bridge story.

Josh McCallen: I'd love to hear your bridge story, your voice is better than mine.

Melanie McCallen: So Josh, of course, was strategically wearing a Renault shirt. And so many doctors and nurses were coming in and discovering the Renault was a wedding venue we ran.

And to make a long story short, about 10 or so brides switched from their previous venues to ours because they discovered we could accommodate them much more quickly with all the push back on dates because of the quarantine. We would explain to them we had so many options with different ballrooms and what not at The Renault, that we weren't crunched for time and space like so many other smaller venues.

We had this amazing nurse Maggie, and she told us her friend was supposed to get married in two weeks but ended up having to move her date to December 11th. And that's when we discovered, wow, we can accommodate them much more speedily than that.

Josh McCallen: Amazing stuff! Another interesting point… And Eric, you and I have been discussing this for some time now: what a great place The Renault is for mastermind groups. And a few days before the baby came we were hosting this elite group of bigger pockets contributors, with Matt Faircloth, J Scott and so on. And they were all talking about coronavirus and thinking, wow, this is really becoming a big topic.

So just a few days earlier, it wasn't more than a topic. And a few days later, we're having the baby and the world's shutting down, and the next day it was just shocking.

Erik Cabral: I have to say, you were also one of my indicators, Josh, because we had just come back from Florida the week before the craze and we were going back and forth. Then the baby came and you said, "Hey, Erik I can't come with you to T & C, this huge conference we had scheduled out months ago and we were going. I was so excited to go.

And I remember, I wrote to you and said, "Why"? And you said, "Coronavirus". It was just that one word: Coronavirus and I was like, wait a minute. I'm like, Oh my Goodness, this is for real. So yeah, it's pretty wild.

Josh McCallen: You are right. Of course, we were planning with Melanie the Learn and Grow Accountable Equity Mastermind for our investors. And we had to postpone that, and we had to cease and desist on so many other things, so it affected everything. The world changed so quickly, it was astounding.

But moving forward, I would say the thing we want to share with the incredible community you and I care about, the Capital Hacking community. That was the beginning. Remember our friend, M.C. Laubscher was telling everybody about the five stages of grief. And at first your—I don't know—disbelief, shock, that's where we all were at that point.

Then there's the negotiation part where you are like we can still have the event a month from now or a week from now. So we were in the middle of that and now where we are today, where it's full blown, we've already had all the national shutdowns. Now we've all, so many of the people you and I spend time with, have decided to make this a power moment; a moment of reflection and a moment of getting ready for the future.

Now is a great time to take into account what you do have and to be grateful for it. And so anyway, I would suggest maybe part of the show today we might talk a little bit about what The Renault did. They did a great job, led by ourselves and Dan Alicea, and the team. They had a wonderful triage program to keep the business safe during this time. We monitor what's going on in our state and every day we follow all the rules. And we are still moving forward with the various facets of construction on our property. Thank God that's still been allowed. Back to the point: right away we started communicating with all our investors.

So every investor knew what we were doing on the asset level. We have a lot more planned. By the way, if you're an Accountable Equity investor, wait til you see all the new things coming in the next few weeks. Melanie will be much more involved as soon as she gets the baby settled at home.

Sure. You can't wait to do some webinars. Right. And to share it. We'll share Coyle on one of the webinars.

Melanie McCallen: Of course.

Josh McCallen: But, Erik, the best part of this from a business point of view, has been that it allowed us all to assess what the heck matters. That's both in family, personal, and in business. And before we get into our family life, which I know you wanted us to probe because of the fact that we have a big family, here is our business life.

With the business, we set up strategy calls two times a week; we outline all the various strategic options for the Renault, both that we had before the Coronavirus and because of the Coronavirus. The strategy for The Renault which is really a national treasure, a gorgeous property is that we need to adjust certain things. So we have a whole list of strategies for doing that, to accommodate the new order of life in this historic moment.

And we're being very seriously intentional about dealing with these issues and using them for strength. Like how can we get stronger because of this? Who else can we serve because of this? And how do we take good care of the people we still have. And also the people we had to furlough, how can we best serve them at this time?

As we're in hospitality and everything got closed, as soon as we're allowed to open, we get them all back. Thank God.

Also, it was important to make sure the team members who had to go and sort of sit on the sidelines for now; that they understand how much we missed them and can't wait for them to come back and be a part of what's going on.

And we're still under construction, but that was scheduled to come to an end right on the heels of all these big weddings about to take off. And so we actually hired, during a great job fair a whole bunch of people, a hundred people or so to really kick off this whole big season of weddings.

It was important to us, we let them know how much we value them, that they're still totally on the team. Everybody had a real excitement about this new Renault that was about to blast off, like a new beginning. This new season, springing out of all the hard work we'd been pouring into and building up for a year. These weddings that were about to be celebrated and the tasting room that was about to open. All of these great things which are like our dreams as a team.

All these awesome events that were about to happen. And then suddenly everyone is on the sidelines. So keeping them in the loop is vital to us. Letting them know things like, you know, what does construction look like? Since we're all sort of sitting at home we want to stay united around that spark of love for this unique business we're in. This business where we serve others in some of the most sacred events of their lives. And to encourage everyone that this is still going to happen. It's just going to happen slowly and differently than we expected.

But there are still brides anxiously awaiting their wedding days and a room that's right on the edge of completion construction-wise. And so keeping that unity, and that spark, and that joy alive until we can make it an actuality again. This is an essential task for us at this time.

Erik Cabral: So I'm curious how you, and I struggle with this. This is a challenge currently with my business and I'm sure others who are listening. What have you implemented to keep the team inspired and engaged?

How do you keep pushing forward and getting everybody excited during these times?

Josh McCallen: Well, let's admit we wish we could do more and we probably have room to grow on this issue. But since you're asking the question, we'll try to answer it humbly. A couple things: we're down to about a tenth of our operating size, so we're a bit smaller. Also, we initiated structured weekly meetings, but obviously on a daily basis we have different rolling meetings.

So we're having a lot of Zoom meetings. And we're intentionally focusing on the goods we can build on. For example, the people that are currently temporarily furloughed. We are bending over backwards to make sure they are accommodated through this time. Finally, it's a matter of fact, we did not let go of our leadership, what we call human capital.

You'd be proud of us. We don't call it HR. We call it human capital, and we have regular communications with everyone. We're striving in every possible way to help those in more need than others. So we're trying to live our mission. In general, I'll tell you, through these sessions we've structured a series of leadership calls that are going to change the way we do business.

And it definitely has fortified us. Construction touch bases every day with all related constituents, including this young lady right here next to me. And then, by the way, if you haven't, go online to the Accountable Equity Facebook page and you'll see beautiful Melanie, right before Corona with baby Coyle in her belly, giving direction to contractors it was awesome. Those are the ways, I would say, we're staying motivated: a lot of face to face zoom and also we're teaching our sales team how to do virtual training. I'm even teaching them about the proximity to the camera that I've been learning, and all those types of things.

But I want to say one other thing. We are, we, Melanie and I, live in two worlds. We have the privilege of being in hospitality and development of hospitality, and the privilege of being in a community of investors. So Accountable Equity, Melanie and I lead together, and we've made this big pivot over the last year and it's all paying off now.

High communication, high community. And that was inspired, you know, Erik you've been part of this from the beginning. From the events we've been holding it became clear to us early on that we wanted to be close to our investor community. We wanted to add value through education and networking, and that I think is going to pay dividends in these changing times for the investors and for us, and all of us collectively as a community. I think it'll add a lot of strength. That's why we're really, really communicating with our community of investors.

Melanie McCallen: I was just overhearing the podcast you had with Bob Wells. Josh McCallen: Yeah I want to compliment Bob Wells and Usha Wells

Melanie McCallen: They're part of our community. And everyone in the community has a great perspective or a little tidbit to share. As you know, many of us in Accountable Equity lived through 2008 and have insight to share because of the parallels... and what could be happening and give calm and just great concrete advice.

So you're just so grateful to be in these circles and everybody's able then to expand their own circles and their knowledge amongst each other.

Josh McCallen: Man, honey, you said it beautifully. Melanie McCallen: Thank you, love.

Josh McCallen: As a matter of fact, I think you should be on more webinars with us. You are good at those!

Melanie McCallen: Coyle's going to have to come, nursing baby has to be with me.

Josh McCallen: People, we are like that! That will be one of the first webinars, with a baby in it, right?

Erik Cabral: It's in his blood and he's a closer, Coyle. Josh McCallen: Coyle the closer, Coffee's for closers Melanie McCallen: No coffee for Coyle

Erik Cabral: Milk's only for closers, Coyle come on! Melanie McCallen: Now we are excited about that.

Josh McCallen: I will add one clarification. We're actually doing more than one specialized group meeting. Every day we're doing at least two a day and they're targeted. For example, on Tuesdays we're doing stimulus.

Decoding the stimulus from the government. We do that twice a week. Then we're having a very small leadership meeting called strategic planning, two times a week. And we're touching base with construction five times a week.

Then once a week, we call the regular leadership meeting, and then on top of that, we're doing a sales team meeting every week. So that's how many meetings we're doing each week. We're breaking them up at different hours, a different audience per meeting.

Sometimes there's overlap.

Clearly, Dan, our Vice President, is part of almost all of them. But we're getting really micro specific on our leadership teams because we don't want to have a meeting ramble. We want a meeting to have a goal. We want to get in and get out, but allow the goal of the meeting to give the discussion long-term value.

Oh, and the other kind of trick we're doing, is when we're in the meetings we take copious notes with Google sheets. We know what we're talking about. We give updates on everything. Every week, every meeting, we're capturing one idea at a time and we're following up on that idea in the future. What I'm saying is the tidbit is one bite size at a time, make progress each meeting, or take motivation from that. And you know us. It's not your idea-my idea, it's always the best idea is what we choose to do. There's a certain humility we all want to strive for right now. What is the right strategy right now? And I think we feel really good about where the strength of the company is.

And you know, a little spoiler alert, we're looking forward to growth through this. Our business has grown during coronavirus because we're a venue that actually has long-term contracts. So we're not in danger. After we reopen, we'll actually have a spike in growth.

Right now, everything is dormant, but eventually we'll be back on track and faster than ever. But how does that position us for acquisition of more properties and more partners?

So, I'm not in any way trying to be contrarian to others here and say we are set up to be a recession proof business. I'm just saying the hard facts reveal that we're looking at a really, really strong future, but we'll need all of us together.

Hey, Eric, I know you and I toyed with this at the beginning, but I have to share with you some of the things Melanie and I are doing as a family for the coronavirus.

Erik Cabral: What are you guys doing? What kind of fun, crazy stuff.

Josh McCallen: Okay, here's what's going wrong for all of us out there that are parents. It isn't going great, I'll be honest with you. But that's okay. Rocky got knocked down, Rocky lost a lot of fights, remember that? He lost a lot of rounds, but in the end he wins. So we're going to win.

Well, we've been knocked down a few times, I think. When you bring a new baby home and on the same day you get about like 25 to 30 emails from different teachers saying, this is what to do, it's a little mind blowing.

Josh McCallen: Yeah, those poor teachers, and they went into immediate email mode, right?

Melanie McCallen: Yeah nobody had a playbook for how to do this. Right? So the teachers were all just trying to figure this out. And so one trick was Josh had each kid get their own email account, even down to Molly, who's in first grade. Even she got her own email account. Then, they themselves emailed the teachers from their own personal accounts and said please email us at these accounts from here on out.

I just couldn't, with that many kids, even begin to keep track of all the information coming in for each one of them. And so that actually really helped. Now they have their own zoom time meetings and they're reminding me and it's kind of like their little job

So Josh saved the day there because I thought it was going to go nuts with that amount of emails.

Erik Cabral: Yeah, no, that was a brilliant little hack there, Mr. McCallen. Melanie McCallen: Yes, it was. That was great.

Josh McCallen: Another cool thing is typing became a fun release for all the kids.

Melanie McCallen: Our kids go to a classical curriculum school, and so technology is way, way low on the list. They'd rather the kids read from original texts and learn.

Josh McCallen: You know, it's a pretty rigorous little school. Melanie McCallen: It's kind of old-school school, you know. Josh McCallen: It's old school.

Melanie McCallen: It's fine with us though because we feel like the kids get plenty of screen time outside of school.

I'd rather them get comfortable using and reading books while they're in school. But that means now with the switch to online, they don't know the keyboard.

And we have rules about screen time but then Josh changed all the rules and their eyes lit up in total joy.

Like you can go on screens at any time, as long as you're playing a typing game. Of course, if I come around the corner, I see screens switched really fast, so I have to assume they've figured out how to get past the rules.

Josh McCallen: sneaky little squirrels...

Melanie McCallen: They figured that out pretty fast.

Josh McCallen: For the most part, it's more like, I would say, rules are fences to herd you. They're not going to change your nature of sneaky squirrelishness. They're moving in the right direction, I would say.

Melanie McCallen: I will say there was a massive uptick in like the amount of food eaten.

You know what I mean? When you're in the house, the kids just think they're hungry all the time because, you know, it's just there.

Josh McCallen: Oh, and by the way, years ago, we designed this beautiful house and Melanie designed an open concept. So, the kitchen is right in the middle of everything. And there's never a time, a little monkey isn't sitting there eating something. And there are so many of them!

Melanie McCallen: I tried so hard to manage it. I'm like, "Kitchen's closed. Give the kitchen a break!"

Erik Cabral: How are you keeping up with your supplies? Do you go to the grocery store constantly, or have deliveries come to the house a lot?

Melanie McCallen: Here's a funny story. Ironically, Josh picked all these movies to watch with our big kids. So the first day I came back from the hospital, Josh went to the grocery store because it was our daughter's birthday and he wanted to get her something special, so he went to the grocery store and called me in a panic, saying, "All of the shelves are empty. I did not realize it was going this bad this fast, and I just talked to somebody here. They said they haven't got an order since Wednesday. What do we need?" I'm like, "Oh my gosh, I just got home literally an hour ago. I haven't been home for two days and I just had a baby. I don't know what we need."

So, he came back home, grabbed two of my kids and went back to BJ's. He had one of them stand in the hour-long line. And then the other one went through the whole store getting huge bags of rice, cans of tuna, peanut butter, and all these huge quantities of bulk canned goods. And this all happened the day I came home from the hospital.

That's Josh for you. He went into Save-the-ship mode. The kids are like, "Yay, we'll never run out of peanut butter. This is great!"

So then that night, I was exhausted. Josh sent me to bed and took charge of the rest of the night. He loves to sit on the couch and have them all cuddled on him.

What movie does he decide the pop in? "Cinderella Man," about the Great Depression. He's like, I better start educating the kids on where we're going here.

Okay. So, then I come down at like 10:00 PM. I'm like, okay, the three year-old probably doesn't understand what's going on. Let's get her to bed.

Josh McCallen: Actually the little ones connected with it. Remember Cinderella man with Russell Crowe, Erik?

Erik Cabral: Yeah,

Josh McCallen: Oh, it's a great movie. And the dad gives up his little piece of fried ham. That was a little girl. My little girls love that scene. I'm like, amen to that!

Melanie McCallen: You would totally do that.

Josh McCallen: We're getting ready for hard times, you know? A few days later I sat down with just the big kids after the little kids went to bed, and they wanted to watch a movie.

Melanie McCallen: So, we throw on "The Hunger Games". A Dystopian future movie! Pretty soon I see a theme emerging through these movie choices.

Anyhow, all that was because you asked us who's going out to get the food. So our oldest, who is a twenty year old woman now. She's in the safer age category and can drive, so we're going to go ahead and let her be the food shopper.

Plus she likes to cook and get some out of the house time. It's just hilarious though, on Facebook there was a picture of Katniss. And the caption compared the person in the family who goes out for food to Katniss Everdeen. And in the picture Katniss is doing the Mockingjay sign. So we're like, Maggie, you're Katniss going out to get the food. And she's, you know, we give her all the gloves and she does all the whole safety thing.

Erik Cabral: Does she make these trips often? I can't even imagine the bill. I mean, it must be hundreds and hundreds of dollars.

Josh McCallen: We can hit a thousand in a week. But you know what? My biggest anxiety wasn't that the economy's not going to be resilient. It was the idea that 350 million of us go out and buy food at the same time and that means you're going to empty the shelves right.

And that's going to create backups. So I thought, you know, we better get the stuff before something like that happens. That being said, hopefully no one thinks less of us.

Melanie McCallen: No, it's hilarious.

Josh McCallen: Anyway we do keep physical distance but not at home.

Melanie McCallen: I'd like to add just one last little thing though, is this really sweet?

So our son Connor is a junior in high school. He's great. And he's got just a great perspective and I attribute it a lot to Josh. He doesn't just see his own small worldview of sort of his high school and what he's doing in his life. He likes to look at the big picture of things.

And he has a lot of gratitude for what we have. And he's a big reader, so he reads a lot of great books and they instill in him even more gratitude.

He's a great kid, but he was so sweet when this whole thing broke out his positive perspective just trickled down to everyone else in the family. So I really am grateful to our kids, and I have to say, having a new baby is really distracting in a great way. As long as they don't watch too much news and surf the internet, with all scary stories. We just strive to stay positive.

And we've been doing family prayers at night. But we do them around a bonfire every night. So that makes it fun for the kids, except for when they call out for s'mores.

Josh McCallen: Oh I hate s'mores.

Erik Cabral: S'mores are the best. I'm glad you guys have a beautiful new life and baby is a good distraction. I wish everybody else had that kind of distraction, including my household, instead of using Tiger King.

Josh McCallen: Yeah.

Erik Cabral: I definitely think you guys have a superior pastime here.

Josh McCallen: Yes, we're blessed with this new little one and we appreciate it.
Erik Cabral: Great stories. I love the lessons learned here.

The silver lining, reflection, family time, building the teams, planning and taking this time to plan and birth. Something new, no pun intended.

Josh McCallen: Lots of pun intended. Melanie McCallen: Lots of fun.

Now back to the Last Life Ever story...

Well, welcome back to the narrative. Melanie is a powerhouse, and we hope each of you readers have the chance to meet her in the future. I am just in love with the lady. There is a very good reason that we co-lead the Accountable Equity company. We want our capital group to be unlike any other in the world. During our first capital-raise, we are proud to say we attracted over $6,500,000 in partner equity. However, the story is not the capital raised, it is the community created. Yes, Accountable Equity took on a new form during our launch. We responded to the voiced and unvoiced yearnings of our partner investors and created a value-add part of our group, we created an Investor Mastermind. What do we mean? We began offering something we call "Investor Hospitality" for prospective investors who wanted to meet us in person and "break bread" with our team. This activity transformed our lives. We started hosting regular "Accountable Equity – Learn & Grow" events at our project properties. Of course, it doesn't hurt that our investment mandate is to invite accredited investors to partner with us and purchase value-add resort properties and turn them into national treasures with strong generational wealth building returns.

Today, Accountable Equity, has over 85 investor families (we love how the wives and the husbands both take pride in the investments we create). This community has become an Investor Mastermind which hosts world-class educational events live at the resort properties four times per year. We welcome you to learn more about the power of investing in private assets rather than public securities in the Wall Street casino, please visit us at www.acccountableequity.com

Yours in Prosperity,
Melanie & Josh McCallen

Josh is a nationally recognized hospitality executive, conference speaker, innovator, builder & investor with a track record for development of exceptional resort properties and growing world-class operational teams.

Melanie is the President of Accountable Equity and also a partner in both Vivamée Hospitality and Accountable Equity, where she manages various designers and architects, as well as serves investors directly. They are the parents of ten (10!!!) children.

TAKE CONTROL OF THE THINGS YOU CAN AND ACCEPT THE THINGS YOU CAN'T.

It was a Friday. I was invited to a company meeting and found myself in a room with two others. One was the head of HR and the other, the head of my department. This would be the last day at my job.

It was a good job. It was a stressful job, but I was good at it. The work I had done was important.

In the first half of my tenure, I found myself leading the engineering team for a software product that managed billions of dollars of inventory every year for distributors across the country. My team was successful, and the product improved.

The second half of my time at the company, I was promoted to a new role of Software Architect. I worked on special projects and was pivotal on a couple of projects of high importance. I was bringing in significant revenue. The end users of my product were very happy. Several publications took note and there was even to be a write-up in Forbes magazine.

Around Christmas time last year, it was announced that the majority share of the company had been sold to an investment firm. A reorganization would change my role. Without warning, I was moved from special teams to under the umbrella of the new team. Without reducing my pay, I was demoted to a regular programmer. Knowing I was overpaid for this new position, I started keeping my eyes open. But for various reasons I felt stuck, it simply was not the right time to make a career move.

The Friday of the meeting, the company that I had shown had some of my biggest successes, chose to move in a different direction; my time there was done. I was told to pick up my things on Monday and that I would be paid up until the end of the month. This amounted to about 3 weeks of severance. Before entering the room, I was a little nervous but when they gave me the news, I was relieved. It had been obvious that the job was no longer a fit for me, and while the company had their reasons for letting me go, they stated that my pay was not in line for what they were now asking me to do; I saw this sudden change as the hand of God giving me a nudge and saying it is not time for you to go. I remember thinking about something I heard from Rabbi Lapin on the radio, how he talked to so many people who stressed about losing their job, how they were so much happier after finding their new one. It was very calming for me.

The meeting was positive. The HR rep was visibly distraught. I said it would be okay and told them to enjoy the weekend. I expressed that I was very proud of my work and that it was fine if this was no longer a good fit for them.

The previous week a friend of mine was let go along with another. I found out later that a handful of others had suffered a similar fate. I have been told that the news didn't go over well with the remaining employees. These decisions may have been hard, or they may have been easy. They may have been wise to the bottom line or they may ultimately turn into a major mistake for the company. I cannot tell and I am not sure it matters. One person told me that I wasn't treated fairly. I appreciated the validation and thanked them for their words but also told them it didn't matter, it was done.

What was most remarkable to me was my calm. For months, maybe even longer I had been living under a cloud of fear and doubt of what might happen. And now that it had, it no longer was nearly as catastrophic as I thought it would be. I clearly saw the hand of God in this. In the Bible it says, "Do not worry." I was always able to do the "worry" part extremely well, it was the "Do not" part that I struggled with.

My rehabilitation started on the way home. The first call was to my wife. She was very supportive, even though it meant more would be on her shoulders. She did critique, "You probably shouldn't have told me over the phone that you were laid off. That would have been better news for you to give me in person." On this point she was probably right. I talked to a recruiter friend of mine a couple of minutes later. He told me about a job opening that I might be a good fit for. Later that day, I talked to a former teammate of mine. He had left soon after I was promoted to an architect. He reminded me of how successful our team had been, and the role that I had had in it. A couple of my closest friends at the company checked on me. Another colleague from a previous job got me an interview at his company. I had a lot of friends that were looking out for me, who were concerned and were eager to help.

During the next week, two things happened. My wife worked a little extra, so I helped with many of the things she normally took care of. I got my daughter off the bus and went grocery shopping. I also brushed up some of my skills so I could be ready for my interviews. As the week progressed, I became excited to get back into a healthy and productive work environment. The market looked good and there were several prospects. My wife also wanted me to take advantage of this time, to regroup and refresh. "It would not come again," she said. She was right.

That Friday, after I was laid off, it was announced that the schools in Michigan would all be closed. It was recommended that people voluntarily stay home because of the recent outbreak of the Coronavirus. Employers were encouraged to have their employees work from home if possible.

I had a race on my hands. My wife and I didn't panic, we tried to act prudently. This was a time for faith. I had to get a job in advance of the big tidal wave. I knew companies were soon going to be less concerned about hiring and more concerned about conserving cash. My wife sequestered me in order to safeguard my health. She worked more to offset the loss of my income and did all of the shopping. We were already trimming down on our expenses from the previous week. I spent additional hours at night studying to improve my skills.

I had a couple of qualifying interviews early that first week. Things were moving forward. One of the companies I was scheduled to interview for decided to postpone interviews and convert their existing staff to remote work. I got a call from an elder at my Church offering help. I returned his call only to find out he was being laid off as well. A couple of my applications came back informing me of hiring freezes and encouraging me to try back when the looming pandemic was over...

The world outside was on fire; however, two job prospects had emerged. I was feeling fortunate that I was in a field that was still in demand. In fifth grade, I remember hearing about workers in the great depression, my teacher said that regular construction workers made a livable wage but could find it difficult to get a job. However, if you had a skilled trade like masonry you had job security and could get a little bit more. I didn't know what it would look like when I grew up, but I wanted to find a skilled trade. This came back to mind during my job search. This is something I remembered while talking to some of my friends who were now also looking for work. It wasn't too long ago everyone I knew had a job. Now the world has changed.

It wasn't until after the first of my final interviews that I truly became nervous, that I began to worry about how long it would take for me to find a job. In one such interview, I found out that there was a hiring freeze but that they were going to continue with the process anyway. The person that I was going to be working with had just quit. The job would become exceedingly difficult, I would be dealing with a technology that I was unfamiliar with and now would be doing it without the benefit of a knowledgeable coworker to show me the ropes. I have been a consultant for much of my career. The job was well outside of my comfort zone and did not include skills that I was interested in developing. Normally, I would say to this potential employer, a strong, "Thanks, but no thanks." Instead, I found myself pressing on saying things like, "I would make a good addition to the team" and that "I would do what I had to do to make this job work and be successful at it." I did not have a good feeling about it, but I didn't feel like I really had a choice.

After that meeting, I called my mom and asked her if we could borrow money. I told her we didn't need anything yet but that we might, and I wanted to know my options. I told her that we would be okay for a month or so but come what May...but would be rough before June. I still had another interview, but that interview kept getting put off because of the interviewer's vacation of all things. I knew at this point that nothing was certain. I may find a job before the Coronavirus ended, but it might mean a substantial pay cut or less than ideal conditions. I was studying, I was applying for work, I was cutting my spending, and taking care of business at home; I felt I was doing everything I could do. It was in God's hands now. I was becoming nervous.

I said a prayer. I was not in control and I needed help. I had to accept my limitations.

Soon after, I got a call telling me that a previous employer was interested in hiring me. This was a real job offer. The pay was comparable to what I had at my previous job. I also had a final interview with a second job as a contractor doing architectural work for a fortune five hundred company. If I got that offer, I would be getting a modest pay raise. Instead of having to settle, I suddenly had my choice of two very good jobs. I accepted the job from my previous employer because it was the right fit for me. It was bittersweet taking that job, knowing so many were out of work. My understanding is that more than 11 million have lost their job in the first two weeks of the shutdown. I had severance until March 31. My first day of work was April 1, my health insurance started that first day. The hand of God...

Here are the lessons I learned:

- Trust God. Remember that He works, even when it seems as if nothing else does.

- Do what you can do and be satisfied with that. Take advantage of the time you are off work and treat it like it is a job. Whether you are new to the marketplace or you have twenty years of experience like I have, continue to invest in yourself.
- Make sure you schedule your time accordingly. For me, it wasn't doing things at a set time, but just making sure I had time budgeted. I had time to be searching for job postings, time to network, time for interviews and time for training. I also needed to make sure I had time for family and helping with the housework. My wife had to remind me of this as my daughter was asking me to play Lego with her. You cannot get time back, so don't waste it.
- Talk with friends and family to get perspective; but remember the decision is yours. Even heartfelt advice may not be the right advice. Poorly articulated advice does not make it wrong. It is up to you to figure out which is which.
- Take stock of those around you. Accept help if you need it. Offer help if you can give it. It's people that make the difference.
- Be satisfied with your efforts. If you are taking the right steps and doing what you can, you are positioning yourself to be ready for the next opportunity.
- Face your mistakes. Don't take on the mistakes of others as your own. At my previous work, I made plenty of mistakes. At the same time, there were times when I took the fall for the mistakes of others. It is good to let the past be the past and move on the best you can. Don't replay past events on what you or they could have done differently as if you can change them. Instead, try to learn from your experiences so they may play-out more favorably in the future. Don't let these experiences jade you, instead become stronger because of them.
- Which brings us back to the first lesson …
- Trust God.

Peter Kotman is a software engineer with more than 20 years of experience. He has worked with companies of all sizes and has been an entrepreneur. Peter is a family man and a man of faith.

LIZ GOLL LERNER

REMEMBERING HOW TO FIGHT AND WIN

I was struck by the speech Queen Elizabeth made a few days ago to her country about this time we are living through: The COVID-19 war.

She said, "I hope in the years to come everyone will be able to take pride in how they responded to this challenge…and those who come after us will say that the Britons of this generation were as strong as any. That the attributes of self-discipline, of quiet good-humored resolve and of fellow-feeling still characterize this country."

Toward the end of her speech she spoke about the world coming together and doing what can be done to defeat this common enemy, knowing that we succeeded in accomplishing this because we all joined in a global effort.

She also said, "We should take comfort that while we may have more still to endure, better days will return…We will be with our friends again; we will be with our families again; we will meet again."

The video of her full speech and a *New York Times* article about it can be found at: https://www.nytimes.com/2020/04/05/world/europe/corona-virus-queen-elizabeth- speech.html?action=click&module=Spotlight&pg-type=Homepage#after-story-ad-1

Much has been said in our country about bravery, about fear, about people moving past fear to do their jobs. Our heroic hospital and healthcare workers showing us what a sense of duty to something greater than ourselves actually means today.

Stoicism and solidarity.

Unless or until we are in the thick of it, solidarity can seem quite quiet and even private. It is only when people are clapping or cheering for the helpers at a certain time every day that it becomes a shared experience of hope.

This is important because while news reports give us important information, headlines also trigger anxiety and it helps to remember you are not standing alone: neighbor in support of neighbor, family member in support of family member, communities in support of businesses and businesses in support of community.

Right now, we are in fact, finding togetherness even when alone.

I love the Queen's speech because it recalled an earlier time when people were expected to use their self-discipline to reach a collective goal or to overcome a hardship. Back then we recognized the importance of our interdependence. Our survival depended on it.

My mother-in-law was a Londoner who came of age during WWII. There was no ego in doing what had to be done but there was pride in the doing.

She, as did many people of her generation, found herself in the thick of the unspeakable. Doing what she could to assist or survive.

For them, it was bombs or persecution. The enemy was quite loud and visible. For us, it is more silent and at times illusive, but we do know what it is.

We need to be sure that we use our wits, think of each other as well as ourselves, find the light at the end of the tunnel and, like the people of an earlier generation, never give up hope.

In short, we must build the muscles we need to thrive in an ever-changing world. This means not becoming our own enemy. Not submitting to apocalyptic thinking.

It is we who will decide what our world will look like going forward. It is we who will decide what kind of family, community, country we want to participate in.

While for a time we will be physically alone, we have the ability like never before to maintain connection and to make these decisions together.

It's not that these ideas or ideals related to our collective power are new. But what is being highlighted now is that we must use those muscles—our collective strength— wholeheartedly and differently.

It can be as simple as having a good attitude rather than one of complaint. Taking our fears and turning them into courage to face another minute, hour, day, in uncertain and, at times, life threatening circumstances.

Now is the time to draw on the strength that has always been there, ready and waiting to be called into action.

Our creativity—our ability to think outside the box—will keep us focused on doing the best we can to make sure our businesses, jobs and relationships thrive. And choosing heart-opening ways to solve differences will help us succeed.

It will all make us more productive and stronger when this crisis is over.

We are seeing now that we have a readiness to do things differently and the capacity required for creating new solutions. There is always an answer when we believe in ourselves and in our collaborators.

In fact, belief in self and in our family members, friends, fellow workers and communities have always been the exact ingredients needed for accomplishing our most treasured dreams.

The Queen was correct: this virus and the weaknesses it has created or exposed, such as leadership, the economy, the environment and more, will be fixed globally. But only if we understand the lesson we're being presented with; only if we come to truly understand and embrace working together.

This was only the fifth time in her 68-year reign that the Queen addressed her nation other than at Christmas. She reminded us that we are made of stronger stuff.

Let's take heed. There is a light at the end of the tunnel, and we can get to it–but only together.

Liz (LCPAT, LPC, ATR-BC), is a counselor, psychotherapist and coach with 30+ years of experience who is nationally recognized as an innovator in the personal growth field for her groundbreaking work in integrative healing. Today, Liz's innovative "Enlightened Communication through Luminous Living" program helps individuals, couples, community groups and organizations navigate high- conflict, high-stakes situations and challenges. Find her at <u>yourinspiredchoices.com</u>

RACHEL ANDERSEN

STRENGTH IN SPIRIT

Dry wind blew over the dusty airstrip as my children and I jogged the 800 yards, enjoying the slightly cooler evening in the desert. Our house lay on the edge of the airstrip and we returned, thirsty and sweaty from our home school PE class. Later that evening friends stopped by, dropping off some satellite internet equipment, which I carried into the house. I couldn't wait until we had an internet connection hooked up. Living in a remote corner of East Africa, we carried on our daily lives without cell phone coverage or landlines. For emergencies we relied on a satellite phone. That evening I would experience the importance of having a way to make an emergency phone call.

In 2008, my husband and I moved to East Africa with five children, ages five and under. I sometimes wonder how we made the decision with those small children. Looking back, I remember the early days of living in Africa as challenging and sometimes frightening. The children did get sick and they got hurt. Sometimes we would run out of groceries and I would have to improvise cooking for a family of seven with limited ingredients.

When I became ill in 2014, our oldest child was at a boarding school, two days drive away, the same town where a major hospital provides service to people from all over Africa. We also had a sixth child, age 4. I was healthy and strong, exercising regularly. I home schooled four children and had learned a second language, Swahili. I had also just begun studying to become a midwife.

The evening we received our equipment for satellite internet, I laid down early while the family watched a movie. I didn't feel that great, and I wanted some rest. After laying around, I checked my temperature, just over 1010 F. I told my husband, Eddie, that I had a fever and asked him to bring something to drink and Tylenol. We had yogurt, and I drank a bit of that.

It wasn't long before I felt worse. I remember hearing God say, "Are you willing to go through this?" I said, "Yes." After that point I don't remember an exact timeline, but I know I began to vomit and that my temperature was climbing. I also distinctly remember telling Eddie what medicine to give me and to start writing down my temperatures. Some of the meds I remember taking were malaria medication, ibuprofen and an anti-emetic (a drug that suppresses vomiting). Much of the night was a blur of vomiting, intense stomach cramps, and passing out.

Eddie faithfully took my temperature and began using cold compresses to try to bring the fever down, alongside of the ibuprofen and acetaminophen. Eddie told me that when he measured my temperature under the arm, it was between 107o and 108o. By early morning, I was delusional and not coherent. The next day I could not understand why my children were running up and down the hallway, getting ready to leave on a plane.

While I was passed out, Eddie made a phone call to a doctor who happened to be in a meeting with several other doctors. They agreed that my condition was alarming and that I needed to be evacuated and admitted into a hospital. They were already trying to sort out what I had. With temperatures as high as mine, they believed I was suffering from cerebral malaria or meningitis. By three in the afternoon, a plane had landed with two doctors on board, and they were ready to take me down.

I was brought to the hospital near our son's boarding school and quickly admitted. IV lines had been placed on the plane and all manner of drugs were soon added to the mix. I lost my hearing for one day due to the medication; thankfully it came back within a day or two after stopping it. I had little physical strength and could not hold any conversation. I remember well, lying in a hospital bed, alone, thinking, "My body is broken, Lord."

They ran all manner of tests and concluded that I likely had a virus. Due to the high temperatures and aching in my neck, my diagnosis was viral meningitis. Although they could not find any evidence of bacterial infection or malaria, I received IV antibiotics and IV malaria meds just in case for five days.

On the fourth day in the hospital my husband brought a book for me which my mother in law had mailed to Kenya, at least a month before I was ill. The name of the book was *Strength for Your Spirit*. In that moment I knew God's hand was upon me. My body was broken and would never be the same. But God promised me strength for my spirit, filling me with hope and peace.

Living in the bush is difficult. Every day is full of unexpected events and changing plans. At heart, I am a planner. I enjoy organizing our travel schedule and booking hotels, guest houses, and AirBNBs for our family. Putting something on the calendar is a way I keep my sanity when all around me the community's needs are unpredictable and chaotic.

We currently have five children who attend boarding school. Three weeks ago, on March 11, our children's school closed two weeks before the end of term. The decision was based on the growing concern that countries across Africa would close their borders, making it impossible for children to be reunited with their families. In an hour, I changed our AirBNB booking, doctor's appointments, and US Embassy appointments. The next day, we packed up ourselves and began the two-day journey to get our kids from school.

Within days of picking up our children, the US Embassy canceled all appointments. We decided to cancel our doctor's appointments and claimed a refund from AirBNB. We bought groceries for eight weeks and headed home. It was easy to laugh that the kids were getting two extra weeks of vacation, assuming we would have an opportunity to reschedule much of our lives.

Last night we were informed that our children's school would continue completely online for the rest of the school year. The US Embassy is closed indefinitely and only available for emergency travel. Our country of service has issued a curfew, closed off most international flights, and is enforcing quarantine for more than 1000 people. Our lives continue to shift daily with each new announcement regarding COVID-19, coronavirus.

Our current situation, fighting a mystery illness, has vividly reminded me of the day when my life changed within hours. Recovery was long, and I have some effects of brain injury. Nevertheless, my spirit is strong. I serve an unchanging God who gives peace, hope, and joy abundantly (Romans 15:13).

The God who allowed me to go through a near death illness also gives me strength for my spirit during this tumultuous time.

We are always dependent on God. During a crisis, this dependence is thrown into our faces and we don't like it. It makes us insecure and anxious, wishing that we could return to the façade of control over our plans. But in the lack of control, we can fall into the arms of a loving Father and rest in His peace.

Each day I need to remind myself to tightly grab hold of the truth and rest in the promises He gives.

Many years ago, I came across a saying, "When worry works, then worry." I have had moments of serious anxiety, barely able to catch my breath, sick to my stomach, and miserable. Research shows us that stress hormones can cause insurmountable damage to our bodies. We must deal with our anxiety in one way or another.

I draw strength from planning, but right now my plans are out of sorts. Planning, which helps me feel less anxious, is not an option for comfort right now. So, I am digging deeper. I spend more time studying what God says about who He is and then choose to believe it. I am accepting that I have idols in my life, and I focus on allowing God to destroy them. The idol of control, lists, and full calendars has been stripped clean. The amazing thing about God is that when he takes away an idol, he is ready to fill it with something else, Himself.

I believe what God says about Himself. I believe He wants me to "abound in all hope." As a midwife, I continue to volunteer at my local clinic. I also find myself uniquely placed to try to provide sensible thought regarding women's health during this time. Giving to others my creative energy and using my resources to help others through this crisis encourages me that all is not in vain. God uses these things to strengthen my spirit.

Most importantly, I can give to others my reason for hope. Knowing Jesus as a Savior and Lord gives me a reason to live that is bigger than making plans or appointments. Knowing Jesus as healer gives me a reason to trust him, to provide healing for people when it is the right thing to do. Knowing Jesus as Father, encourages me to cast my anxiety on him because He cares for me (I Peter 5:7).

Each day is a challenge right now. News headlines and political pundits do not encourage me to have peace or to have hope or joy. In the middle of my brokenness, I can have strength for my spirit through Christ. I can abound in all hope.

Rachel Andersen and her family live in Northern Kenya with their six children, ages 18-9. Their location is six hours of two track road from the closest pavement in rugged desert. They work among people who herd camels, cattle, goats, and sheep, serving them through well drilling, midwifery, radio ministry, and multiple other projects.

JOANNE STARK

REFLECTIONS ON LIFE AND COVID-19

One little mysterious parasite has stopped the world. The pause button has been pressed on our everyday lives, as the news shouts out the mounting statistics of COVID-19 cases and deaths. Where do we find the inner strength and resources to get through this?

If you've lived to be 70, as I have, you've probably encountered other times in your life where you searched for a light in the darkness, tried to find the tools, insights, and people to point you in the right direction.

I thought of how my everyday life had in fact disappeared before. **What Was I Thinking? I Guess I Wasn't.**

> *"I'm very aware, but I'm very naïve. When you are really naïve and expecting safety and expecting the best, you don't feel you're taking risks. You can get smacked a little, but usually it works out pretty well."*
> – Shirley MacLaine

When I was 22 years old, I packed my bags and boarded a plane with 100 other Peace Corps volunteers - destination Africa. When I opened the acceptance letter telling me I was going to Zaire, a former Belgian colony, (now the Democratic Republic of the Congo), the first thing I said was, "Where's that? I don't care, I'm going."

I had heard Africa was amazing. Colonization by European countries had kept the African countries undeveloped and the people uneducated. In fact, there was only one college graduate in all of Zaire at the time I arrived. I would teach the African youth English. They would go onto universities, get great jobs and bring Zaire out of poverty.

I would write a book, work for the UN, and happily live in a world as portrayed in one of the peaceable kingdom paintings of Edward Hicks.

I had never bothered to find out about the reality of life under certain African dictators or the reality of living conditions in third world countries. No historical perspective, no facts to support my utopian delusions.

And so, I did indeed get smacked a little. Before even arriving in Zaire, our group was detained in Uganda by President Idi Amin, known as the "Butcher of Uganda". The United States didn't have diplomatic relations with the country at the time and Amin accused us of being spies. We were held captive for four days. I had no idea that Amin did not hold human life as sacred – kind of like the virus. Initially, not understanding the seriousness of the situation, our group made the grave mistake of trying to interact with some of the guards. Those that returned the kindness were jailed, and perhaps killed.

We, too, may well have lost our own lives. It took the intervention of Mobutu, President of Zaire, at the bequest of President Nixon, to get us freed.

There was also the question of how to prevent getting malaria. We were given a daily medication just for that purpose. My school was in the second largest city in Zaire, Lubumbashi. I didn't know anyone with malaria; it wasn't rampant in my neck of the forest. I forgot about taking the pills. I made it through a year free of the disease. Then one day I turned a horrible shade of gray; I was burning hot and sweating, then shaking from an internal arctic cold, nausea, vomiting, pain. Symptoms came back for years.

These were hard ways to learn the dangers of being superficially informed and accepting what I wanted reality to be rather than the truth.

I was as guilty of negligent naiveté as those young adults on spring break who packed the beaches in spite of the early warnings about the virus, the purveyors of the hoax nonsense, or those thinking they were immune for whatever reason.

"But I was so much younger then, I'm wiser than that now."
— Bob Dylan

FEAR NOT

"You gain strength, courage, and confidence by every experience in which you really stop to look fear in the face. You are able to say to yourself, "I lived through this horror. I can take the next thing that comes along."
— Eleanor Roosevelt

When I was 27, I got a job with Bell Helicopter and headed to Iran, fresh out of graduate school to work on an English curriculum for Iranian helicopter pilots. Mohammad Reza Pahlavi, the last Shah of Iran was on the throne; the wealthy, powerful American ally who embraced western values. Life was good in Iran. I had to dress conservatively, but could go out on my own without wearing a chador. Days were filled with international friends, fine food, and Armenian wine. We lived in an old house with two-foot thick walls, high ceilings, and a flower garden with a small pool in an old part of Isfahan.

Iran was still a Muslim country, of course. We heard the call to pray several times a day from the mosque down the block. There were many devout Muslims waiting for the return from France of the exiled Ayatollah Khomeini, who had been fanning the flames of a revolution for years.

It all ended when the Shah was diagnosed with cancer and left the country. The revolution had begun. It was dangerous to be an American. Our house was at the end of a small cul-de-sac. At eight o'clock every night the lights went out. We pulled the drapes closed, lit a candle and listened to the news from the BBC on our battery- powered radio, while gunfire erupted in the streets. One night, the crowd emptied into our alley, yelling "Death to the Americans". We called the consulate and asked to be rescued. We were told it would be more dangerous for us if they tried to send someone in to save us. I sat in the dark in my nightgown, holding a kitchen knife. It was the first and only time in my life that my knees have uncontrollably knocked. The crowd finally dispersed; but we knew they'd return the next night. Stay and hope or do something?

We moved out of our conservative neighborhood the next day into one of the many vacant apartments in a safer part of the city. The apartment was owned by a man of the Baha'i faith who volunteered to do our grocery shopping. I went with him, not wearing a face mask, but a chador. We were evacuated a few months later; the day Khomeini returned from exile.

I had realized that the way to mitigate the fear was to pray for guidance, assess the situation and act.

*"Don't have a spirit of fear, but of power
and love and a sound mind."*
− 2 Tim 1:7

WE HAVE THE TOOLS

Of course, there is not a one size fits all answer for finding your way to a place of safety, sanity and peace during this time. We each need to rely on our faith, tap into our strengths and seek out the wisdom of others.

What do I know? The enemy is not only the virus but anxiety, depression, sadness, isolation, and uncertainty. This is no time for naiveté, it's no time to be paralyzed by fear, it's no time for inaction.

We are all experiencing different levels of worry, need and loss. How we respond should match our own personal realities. All we can do is deal with the Now in light of our capabilities and necessities.

I have COPD, I'm 70. I have control only over a small part of the big picture. It comes down to who we are, where we are, what we need, what we can give.

I can pay my cleaning lady even though she can't be here. I can increase my donations to our charities. I can reach out to others whom I know aren't coping well.

There are the obvious things we should all do: eat, exercise and sleep well, help financially, budget resources, be grateful for the people in our lives and the homes in which we shelter, wear masks and greet and smile from 6 feet away.

I have no profound wisdom to impart. But there is an arsenal of tools out there to help us. Here are a few of mine.

PRAYER, YOGA, MINDFULNESS

Prayer is powerful. We all find our own way of relating to that which we deem greater than ourselves. You can talk to God or the Universe, sing to Him, read about Him or breathe into the silence. I am a practicing Episcopalian, I read the bible, say novenas, pray the rosary, and say the Lord's Prayer while I sanitize my hands. I also practice Yoga and try to be mindful when I start to lose it.

I recently read the advice from a Hopi indigenous Shaman, White Eagle. He says that during this time, we can either go down the hole of 24-hour news, nervousness and pessimism or through the portal to new life and serenity in the storm. Take this opportunity to look at yourself, rethink life and death, take care of yourself and others. Do not lose the spiritual dimension of the crisis. Calm down and pray every day, preferably at the same time; sing, dance, resist through art, joy, faith and love. Don't feel guilty about feeling happy. Good things need to emanate from the universe.

Thank you, White Eagle.

COPING AND CONNECTING

In the New Yorker magazine, Augustin Fuentes, an evolutionary scientist at Notre Dame University, discusses how important it is to not isolate and to reach out in creative ways. In his article, "Finding Connection and Resilience During the Coronavirus Pandemic", he references a number of interesting examples from across the world. Hong Kong has started a new reality show called 'Home Karaoke Station" where famous singers perform viewer's songs while in quarantine in their own homes. In Iran, there is a show where viewers send in their videos to participate in dance challenges. It's worth a read.

As for me, I am continuing my French class using WhatsApp and my yoga class on Zoom.

BOOKS

Get lost in another time and place. I'm reading" The Amazing Journals of James Taylor" (not that James Taylor). It's a fictional book which takes place in the period of history following the Civil War. "…a gripping story of adventure, crime and punishment, mystery, love and disappointment, hard work and devotion to the principles of human strength and moral dignity."

MUSIC

I have been listening to John Rutter's "For the Beauty of the Earth" and "Look at the World". These are beautiful choral works that touch the soul.

OLD PHOTOS

A walk down memory lane. Old photos bring back memories of happy times, and people I haven't thought about in years. I've even looked at my old yearbook. Sweet nostalgia.

WORDS OF WISDOM

"If you are going through hell, keep going. Never give in, never give in, never, never, never, never — in nothing, great or small, large or petty — never give in except to convictions of honor and good sense. For myself I am an optimist — it does not seem to be much use being anything else."
– Winston Churchill

"If light is in your heart, you will find your way home.
– Rumi

"Fear is the path to the dark side. ..."
– Yoda

"And once the storm is over, you won't remember how you made it through, how you managed to survive. You won't even be sure, whether the storm is really over. But one thing is certain. When you come out of the storm, you won't be the same person who walked in. That's what this storm's all about"
– Haruki Murakami

This too shall pass and I believe good will come of it. The broken parts of society are being revealed. Let's hope a new personal and societal humanity evolves and we develop a lasting strength to help us weather any storm.

Joanne Stark is a retired instructional designer. She served two years in the Peace Corps in Zaire as an English teacher and worked for Bell Helicopter in Iran writing training material for Iranian helicopter pilots and mechanics. She lives in San Diego, CA

LIBBY & MIKE FLOWERS

WORSHIP IS NOT SUSPENDED UNTIL FURTHER NOTICE!

"In an effort to flatten the curve and to keep our health care system from being overwhelmed with cases of Covid-19, I am directing all face to face worship services, Bible studies and church meetings suspended until further notice." This is an excerpt from an email the Bishop of our church sent at the beginning of the encroachment of the Corona Virus into North and South Dakota. When I first read these words, I was in shock that transitioned to extreme sadness and then anger. In the course of five minutes, I had experienced three of the seven stages of grief. Later, I would experience the depression that comes with uncertainty and fear. Life as I knew it was taking a radical twist. How was I going to continue sharing the gospel of Jesus Christ with the peoples in our congregation and community? After all, Ministry is about relationship building and getting close to people. if we can't meet face to face, how are we going to support each other? I began to speak with other pastor in my peer group to see how they were feeling and how they were going to deal with not meeting face to face. Ideas began to float around as we talked about video recordings, Facebook live and ZOOM. I came away from those conversations with a feeling of hope that we could continue, not as usual, but we could continue. It would be a different experience for us as we learned new skills and ways to reach out to our community. As I began to prepare for the first Sunday worship, I began to feel better about our situation. Delving into my Bible and researching my next Sunday message brought a normalcy to my life and my mood began to change from depression to hope that this could work. We could actually worship together even though we were apart. On Sunday afternoon I set my iPhone and notes on a music stand to prepare to share worship with…an empty room. I was struck by the stark emptiness of that room and felt the sadness begin to creep in on me as I looked out at what just the week before had been full of children and adults sharing songs and words of hope in a communal worship. I began my weekly "ritual prayer" of clearing my mind and centering my thoughts and the sadness began to lift. As I began worship with the announcements, the opening prayer and a song, I began to feel the comfort of just being in worship. I will admit, it felt strange to preach to an empty room, but just knowing that these prayers, songs, and words would soon be shared with our community on our Ministry Facebook page, Messenger, text and email made me feel hope. I always end our worship with an encouraging word, and I will always remember the words from that first video worship; "May God's light shine so brightly in our lives that others see him in us!" I hit the end button and sighed in relief that I had gotten through this first "New" service. After sharing the video on the various social media platforms, I soon realized the benefits of sharing worship with a broader audience as people who have never been to our church were now viewing our worship service online! We were getting comments from folks in our community that were not aware we had services and from friends hundreds of miles away who are connected to our ministry through our mission programs. What I thought was going to be a futile effort in sharing the gospels of Jesus Christ with our congregation exploded on social media to include over 200 individual views on our page! Friends of our page began to share the service on their own Facebook pages and we were receiving words of encouragement and hope from people we have never met. The forty some members of our congregation were now reaching out to hundreds of other people. This gives me hope for the future and we will from this point forward, video record our services to continue to reach out to those who are not able to participate in person.

Our ministry also manages and runs a food pantry for those in our community who have food insecurities. Our previous policy has been to allow the customers the ability to free shop in the pantry and select those items they like and need the most. The physical distancing recommendations have forced us to have a drive-up service with pre-boxed groceries that we load into their cars for them. We are now seeing a need for more cleaning and sanitizing products. When a friend heard of these needs through our social media outreach, she immediately began raising funds to help with the purchase of these types of items. We are now able to provide many in our community the necessary items combat the virus that is Covid-19. I am always amazed by the goodness in others and the way God works through them to bring small miracles to our ministry.

Our congregation heard of the need for non-medical face masks and jumped into action. The ministry purchased three sewing machines and the needed supplies to make masks. In just three days, three of our members sewed over 250 masks and we delivered them to family and other members of our community. We are now planning a community garden to help with providing fresh vegetables for the pantry and elder feeding programs on the reservation. They have taken this challenging time and met it with strength and hope for the future.

I am so proud of the way everyone has come together, even though we are apart, to affect the peoples of our community and beyond. My feelings of disbelief, sadness and anger have been replaced with joy and hope for our future as a congregation, ministry, community and world. Take a moment to see the good in others and remember to always love God and love neighbors. May our creator blow the breath of His Holy Spirit on you that you may feel His presence and give you hope and peace.

Pastor Mike Flowers and Libby have been missionaries on the Spirit Lake Nation in North Dakota since February 2007 and are co-directors of the Spirit Lake Ministry Center. They facilitate justice and mercy ministries along with worship, Bible studies and children programs for the people of the Spirit Lake Nation.

HOW TO CREATE CERTAINTY IN UNCERTAIN TIMES

There are 2 things in life happening for us and against us. Those 2 things are the controllables and the uncontrollables.

There is nothing you can do about the uncontrollables. They are going to happen to you, whether you like them or not. The thing about uncontrolables is that you can't control them. That being said, they shouldn't matter to you.

What should matter are the things you can control. Which is what I want to focus on and make the purpose of this chapter. We can focus on the things we can control and that will help us get better certainty in our lives.

So what are the things you CAN control in uncertain times?

#1 YOUR ATTITUDE

You can control how you choose to deal with tough times. You can choose the mindset you need to adopt in order to make it through tough times.

I was locked up in prison for 3 years of my life in my 20s. I had no control over the fact that I was locked down. What I could control was how I chose to act while locked down, and what I did with my time while locked down.

As I write this, we are ALL on lockdown in quarantine over the coronavirus of 2020. I'm going to give you some tips on how to keep a good attitude when you are locked down against your will.

First off, you need to search for things to be grateful for. After all, I was locked down with murderers and rapists, now I'm locked down with my wife and kids. I'll take my wife and kids over the bad guys any day of the week. I'm grateful that I get to be locked down with people I love instead of people I can't stand.

I'm also grateful that I'm healthy, safe and unconcerned with whatever the bigger picture behind all this is. I'm not worried if we are going to war, 5G is being installed or the lizard people from the underground are here to take us over. I could care less about what's really going on. I'm choosing to be grateful that I'm not consumed with the rabbit holes filled with conspiracies that are out there. I'm focused on being grateful for being alive and well.

Every morning when I wake up, I write down multiple things that I am grateful for:

- My health
- My family
- My friends My job
- My clients
- My ability to stay focused on the positive

When you get focused on the right things, the right things happen. You can guess what happens when you focus on the wrong things.

#2 WHAT YOU DO WITH YOUR TIME

While on lockdown, you have extra time. After all, you don't have to drive to work, you don't have to drop kids off at school, you have extra time to learn, grow and expand your mind.

Right now is the time to get back into being healthy. Being healthy consists of 2 parts. Diet and Exercise. When you start working out and eating right (things you can control) your quality of life gets better. This is just one of the ways you can spend your time wisely.

Another thing you can do with your time is to get educated. You can learn a new skill, read a book, take a course and even learn how to get Government grants and things like that. If you have extra time, you might as well make the most of it.

The vast majority of people will be watching Netflix, drinking heavily and sedating themselves with mindless activities that do them no good. You can control how you spend your time and it's up to you to make the most of it.

#3 LOVING THOSE WHO MATTER MOST

Who you focus your time on matters most. Right now is the time to love your family more. Stay in contact with your closest friends, and take care of those who take care of you.

The world needs more love right now. You can either contribute to the supply of love needed, or you can be just another person who is caught up in anger and frustration. Trust me, the world doesn't need one more ounce of anger and hate. It needs more love. Supply is down, which means you have a demand you can fill.

We are running into a brick wall right now but before you run into the wall, stop and look at it. If you look close there's a note on that wall that reads, "Everything is working for your benefit, if you choose to let it" most people think things are happening to them, in reality, things are happening for them.

We live in the best time to be alive and this minor setback, like many before it, can be overcome with you focusing on the right attitude, the right use of your time and the right people.

Creating certainty is what the world needs you to do right now. We don't need more people adding fuel to the inferno that's ablaze at the moment. We need someone who can help extinguish that fire.

You can help put the fires ablaze out by being the voice of reason, the voice of certainty and the person who motivates and inspires the people in your sphere of influence, no matter how big or small your circle may be.

Warren Buffett once said, "When others are greedy, be fearful and when others are fearful, be greedy." What he was trying to elaborate on is that when everyone is doing one thing, do the other.

Right now everyone is being scared, uncertain and worried. You need to be brave, certain and have a plan. That's what a true leader does in times of turmoil. You are the leader we need right now.

THERE ARE 2 TYPES OF LEADERS

The natural-born leader is born to lead. These are people like Donald Trump, Barrack Obama, JFK and more. These guys have been leaders their entire lives on one level or another.

The situational leader is someone who was not born to lead, but the situation they are in makes them step out of their comfort zone and step up to be a leader. I think Moses is the best example of this. He wasn't born to lead, but he led the Jews into an entire new world.

You may not be a natural-born leader, but the situation we are currently in is forcing those who have it in them to step up and be situational leaders.

Controlling what you can control and doing what you need to do is all it takes to be a leader. When you create certainty in your own life, others will take your lead and follow it.

The fact that you're reading this means you are looking to help yourself get through this trying time on our planet. This makes you a leader. You are doing your best to lead yourself out of the frenzy and because of that, others will follow you.

You can only be certain of what you can control and when you focus your efforts on what you can control, the things you can't control no longer matter.

My goal in this chapter is to give you clarity on what's needed, how you can fill the need and ultimately become someone of influence who can lead those around you by example.

Keep your head up, keep your attitude in check and stay focused. I don't make promises I can't keep and I promise you we will all come out of this on the other side better than we went in.

I'll be praying for you, just like I pray for everyone else. You got this. Just take the lead.

Ryan Stewman is a reformed convicted felon that turned his life around, found Jesus, and trains people on how to expert salespeople through his Hardcore Closer program. Ryan is a 4x Best Selling author and contributes To Forbes, Entrepreneur, Addicted2success, Good Men Project, Lighter Side of Real Estate, and Huffington Post.

HOWLING AT THE MOON

The other night was a pink moon, the biggest, brightest full moon of the year.

I'm kind of a nerd for such things, so I broke my shelter-at-home order and went outside to have a gander.

The sun was mostly down and the moon was on the horizon. Boy, was it a sight to behold. I stood there in awe, mesmerized by its beauty.

Then, I was caught off guard by what sounded like a dog howling. Then another. Then another. But it wasn't dogs... It was my neighbors.

The couple from across the street was on their porch, howling at the moon. The neighbor kids from three houses down were doing the same thing. In fact, I could hear people howling all over the neighborhood. What the heck was going on?

I texted my friend Tasha, who lives on the other side of town. She said they were doing the same thing in her neighborhood. In fact, it had been going on for the last couple of nights.

Apparently, some people from Colorado had started a group on Facebook, were they all pledged to howl at the moon every night at 8 pm. Within a couple of weeks, the idea had spread halfway across the world. We just happened to be lucky enough to live in the epicenter of where it all started.

We've seen a lot of stories like this popping up over the last couple of months. People in Italy singing from their balconies. People in Brooklyn rapping to Biggie lyrics. People coming together, even while having to stay six feet apart.

For the last few weeks, I've watched fear and stress bring out the worst in people. We've all seen YouTube videos of people fighting over toilet paper rolls. We've seen pictures of empty meat walls posted on Facebook. We've heard stories of New York emergency rooms looking like war zones.

But to be there in that moment, to hear the neighbor kids howling and to see their parents smiling, it was magical, to say the least.

I try to see the best in people, even when they prove me wrong. I try to look for the silver linings, even when it's pouring outside. I try to be thankful for my blessings, even on the crappiest of days. But I'd be lying if I said it was easy, especially in the middle of all this.

People are confused. Even the experts keep changing their advice and predictions on a day to day basis. All that confusion, stress, and fear can take a toll on you. I know it's taken a toll on me.

When the people who watch the news finally figured out that something was happening, our local stores turned into mad-houses. I expected this to happen; that's why I did my preparation shopping about three weeks before. But to watch it happen was like something out of a Hollywood blockbuster movie.

Night after night of watching the news didn't make things any better. Fear. Fear. Fear... And now a word from our sponsors. At a time when we need to keep our immune systems strong, it seems like the media is doing everything they can to keep us stressed out and immuno-compromised.

And in the middle of all this, I have Bella; my 10-year-old stepdaughter who can't understand what's going on. "I hate CoronaVirus," she tells me. And it breaks my heart to hear it.

For her, I have to stay strong. For her, I have to set an example. For her, I have to make sure she stays protected, both physically and emotionally.

What I show her is what she'll expect as normal when she gets older. If I let stress get the best of me and allow myself to lash out, she'll find that acceptable from the people in her life as she ventures out into the world. If I let my fear overcome me, she'll learn it's okay to let her fear overcome her. These are not the lessons I want to be teaching her.

I want her to be adaptable. I want her to always be able to find the bright side of things. I want her to remain strong in the face of adversity. And I want her to know it's not okay to let your emotions rule you.

These are things I've always tried to teach her; leading by example whenever I could. Going through this pandemic, I have to admit, it's been more difficult than usual. But I'm hanging on... We both are.

Bella goes out and howls at the moon, every night now. You can hear howls from five blocks over, probably more. It's one of those things that let her know she's not alone, even though it feels like that at times.

Just today, we started opening back up the state. "Safe-at-home" is what they call it. We took advantage and went out for a walk as the sun was going down.

People were out, walking the neighborhood, respecting each other's distance, but beyond happy to get some interaction. Everyone we passed smiled, waved, or said hello. The difference from before was undeniable.

Our neighborhood is upper-middle class and most people tend to mind their own business. You might get a nod every now and then, but rarely anything more than that. Today, people couldn't wait to show you how happy they were to see you.

The little things we take for granted - toilet paper, human contact, a hug from a loved one - these things are all more valuable in a post-COVID reality. And I hope we're not quick to forget their importance.

As the world gets more digitized, the technology that brings us together has also torn us apart. We can all be at the same dinner table, but each one of us off in our separate worlds. But all it took was a simple howl at the moon to remind me that we're not alone... that we are a community... and we are in this together.

In closing, I would ask this of you:

1. Take stock of your blessings and be grateful.
2. Remind yourself of why you fell in love with your partner, and tell them.
3. Find a reason to compliment your co-worker, and do it.
4. List the reasons you're proud of your children, and give them some praise.
5. Life is short. You may not get a second chance to let the people you love know just how much they mean to you.
6. Life can also be hard. And when you do the things listed above, you'll make it a little easier for the people around you.
7. Count your blessings. Be a blessing.

Nathan Fraser is a marketer and direct response copywriter, living in Colorado. He spends most of his time writing sales pages and hanging out with his family. When not doing that, you can find him stirring the pot on social media.

HEIDI RAU

A NEW KIND OF NORMAL

It probably is not far fetched for me to say that I likely speak for the majority of the population when I say that these last few weeks have been more than an uncomfortable adjustment for most of us. Those of us with children are suddenly homeschooling and learning to appreciate the dedication of our teachers. Most of us are now having to cook three meals a day, learning to appreciate the freedom and convenience of eating out. We are all looking for ways to occupy our time at home without succumbing to "cabin fever." It is starting to give us all a better understanding of the word "freedom" as many of our everyday freedoms are temporarily postponed from our "everyday."

What we are currently facing together as a society is the threat of a terrible virus on our families and communities. There is a silent world war wreaking havoc across nations, where the only weapon is an organism capable of taking out a mass percentage of our overall population. These grim thoughts are plaguing our nations with anxiety on a daily basis. This has become the new normal. It does not care how old you are, how rich you are, whom you voted for, what your religious beliefs are, or the color of your skin. I find it ironic, that amidst all of our differences it has taken this virus to make us all understand just how alike we all are.

The shock factor of it all has especially notable significance, as most of us did not plan to have our lives flipped upside down overnight. We are combatting a serious illness on a global scale. In essence, the world is sick, and as a result our daily lives have been temporarily disrupted with no clear end date. The future seems filled with much uncertainty, and we commonly complain that we are just ready for things to go "back to normal."

This idea of us all going through a serious illness together and wishing for things to get back to normal created a pretty humbling experience for me personally. My father being a two-time cancer survivor has seemed relatively cool through all of this. His second bout with cancer was a rather rough one that put him into a state of being immuno-compromised for the rest of his life. My mother is constantly worrying about him with the current climate. However, my father seems rather unaffected by the mass panic. What I came to realize was this – my father has already had to put his life on hold twice with less than hopeful prognoses each time. Whereas, the rest of us are sick with worry about what is to come and are complaining about having to put our lives on hold, there are people out there that have already had to do this due to terminal illness. Looking at it from that perspective has really given me a greater appreciation for what we consider "normal" life, as mundane and cumbersome as it may seem at times. True freedom is held in the foundation of health.

It is my true belief that things will go back to normal someday, but it will be a new kind of normal. Things will not normalize until everyone understands that this is a time for rest and reflection. It is time for us to stop and listen to what the earth and wind are saying. Listen to what God's creatures are saying, and how joyful they are without us constantly in their way. Let them have their time, and when we are ready to join them with a mindfulness approach of love, kindness, and care this virus will no longer be an issue for us.

We as humans, and especially as Americans, are constantly on the go. We are inundated with information thrown at us at a constant pace. We live in a society of instant gratification. Not only has this significantly changed our perception and expectations of the world, but it has also been an incredible distraction. We live our lives plugged in and turned on, and it has been exhausting us more than we realize. These distractions debilitate us from being the best versions of ourselves. We are always too busy to slow down and open our eyes to life going on without us.

For me personally, I have started to gain a greater appreciation for having a moment to slow down and breathe. My kids are now 3, 5, and 12. They have literally been growing up right under my nose, and I can recognize that amidst the hustle and bustle of everyday life I have not given myself the time to cherish that. These last few weeks have given me time to reflect on the fact that I am raising little humans. They are little sponges that learn how to be adults from their parents. I feel like it is important for us all to consider if how we have been doing things is what we want for our children someday. Do we want them to become overly consumed with less meaningful relationships and more information than they can handle? Or do we want something better for them?

I believe most parents would agree that their biggest desire for their children is for them to be self-sufficient. This seems to be an eye opener on helping us realize just how much we have not been practicing what we preach. Is self-sufficiency fighting with others over the last roll of toilet paper in the store? Is self-sufficient purchasing more groceries that you could ever possibly need at any given time? Reflection - how can we live more sustainably? Washcloths over toilet paper? Vegetable gardens? The garden center was absolutely packed to the rims when I stopped in a few days ago. This is a sign that people are starting to wake up to that; that we all need to learn how to be more self sufficient to minimize the impact of disruptions in our everyday routines. I have also seen multiple chicken coops going up across neighborhoods. This is an easy one because what is another of the "firsts" to go at the grocery store during panics? Eggs, of course. The point is, by relying too much on anyone but ourselves we have put ourselves at a serious disadvantage.

It is important during this time to nurture relationships. In my attempts of doing so, I have been having quite a few FaceTime calls with friends I was overdue on catching up with. One of these calls in particular was with two of my long-term friends Jen and Beth. We decided that if we were not going to have the chance to see each other in person, we could still "hang out" on a group call. This world may be shutting us in but not shutting us out from having amazing support for each other's sanity through all of the chaos. Taking us back to the time when conversations were made on meaningful heartfelt phone calls again and having a genuine interest in what is being said on the other line. We stayed on that call talking with each other for three hours. Talking about hopes, fears, dreams, and the future. What I came to realize after that call was that phone calls have been mostly replaced by our use of social media. Phone calls used to mean a lot more when I was a kid. It was the only way we could really keep up with what our friends and family were doing when we were apart. However, times have changed that and now rather than having an hour long phone call conversation with a friend or family member, we spend hours getting little glimpses of everyone's lives on our Facebook News Feed.

I think what we are finding in our current climate is just how much physical social interaction is important to us. It's as if we have found ourselves in a naturally occurring social experiment amidst utter disaster. Though we may be interacting much more with each other on social media platforms to still feel connected with one another, it simply just doesn't satisfy our innate desire for real human interaction. I feel that this is a time when we can step back and realize just how much we all need each other, regardless of all of the divides there are between us. We all mean something and we are all hurting in unique ways that fall along similarities here and there. The majority of experts have already agreed that the constant information, namely with social media, has caused a greater mental health crisis than not. So in a time when our collective mental health is at stake with the uncertainties surrounding us, I encourage all of you reading this to take a step back. Take a hiatus from social media and constant news programs. Come up with a good list of people, maybe your top 10. Dedicate a phone call a day to each of them. Day 1, your number 1, day 2 your number 2 and so on. I promise you that this interaction will be much more meaningful and beneficial to your mental health than throwing 20 or so likes and comments plus 5 posts on your social media every day. Then fill in the time in between doing something productive. Maybe working on that garden or organizing your home office for the first time ever. If you are a parent, get your kids involved in the more productive activities. We have to remember their mental health has to be nurtured as well.

We have all been guilty of making unproductive uses of our time. It seems that over the years people have gotten relatively nastier towards each other, quite often saying things online that they would not dare say to someone if they faced them in person. We have wasted so many hours arguing and calling each other names, all in the want and desire to be "right." Though I have still seen things like this happening in my news feed during this time, it seems that everyone is finally taking a step back and slowing down a little. There is a change happening. People are beginning to post more positive and supporting posts. We are beginning to get outside more and tending to our gardens. We are using more of our time to do things that matter rather than those which tear us apart. It has literally taken a virus to unite us. This is something we should be paying close attention to as a society. This is something we need to open up our eyes to. This is something that gives us the opportunity to stop and think and make a decision on what we are going to do differently on the other side of all of this, and how we are going to make our own little corners of the universe better places to live to contribute to the greater good.

The earth is healing, and we all need to utilize this time to slow down and heal ourselves. The birds sang today like I have never heard them sing. There are less of us on the roads these days destroying the air. We aren't all in a rush anymore. We are all taking a step back, and in the process of protecting ourselves and families we are letting the earth HEAL. If you could only step outside and behold the beauty in that..really appreciate what is happening outside.. really listen to the living creatures around you rejoice..I promise you will find peace in this trying time. It is time for us all to open our eyes and have an inner dialogue with ourselves on what we are going to do to come together and make this world a better place on the other side of this. We have to make a decision today of what we are going to do differently when we wake up to keep those birds singing like this. This is the most humbling experience for us all to understand and appreciate our own personal freedoms that we most generally take for granted. For relationships we take for granted. For a planet filled with absolute natural beauty we take for granted. I love each and every one of you reading this message. In the midst of it all, we are all tied together as the human race and are completely capable of loving each other with compassion and without conditions. We are all capable of empathetically appreciating the life that exists around us in all of creation. It is a time for rest and a time for reflection. Find your purpose.

> *Heidi Rau – Mother, Dreamer, Realtor, Actress, Writer, Queen of my own little kingdom*

WHERE TO FIND HOPE

Our family has seen its fair share of struggle. We have been down and out, kicked around, and dragged through the mud more than once. We married early (I was barely out of my teenage years) and within six months we had our first son. Not having finished college first we were in a position of working blue collar jobs and living paycheck to paycheck. I worked in factories, drove a truck, and eventually started my own small construction company. We were never rich by American standards.

With this context, living paycheck to paycheck, we were always one surprise away from financial difficulty. In fact, there were at least three times in our life where I seriously considered bankruptcy. I do not share this to justify any decisions I made or to stir up any sympathy, only to show you that we know difficulties. With these types of stress come battles against anxiety, depression, and despair.

It was in the midst of one such season when my wife spoke to me words of wisdom that would stay with me forever. One thing we have always tried to do, though we are far from perfect and often lack consistency, is family devotions after dinner each night. This had been a difficult week. Within the matter of a few days I lost my job due to downsizing, both of our vehicles died on us each with expensive repairs, and one of our five children was getting sick. I was at the end of my rope.

We try to maintain the habit of reading consecutively through whole books of the Bible. This makes it more difficult to skip hard passages and forces us to think contextually through the Bible. We were currently reading through the book of Romans. On this particular evening we had come to Romans 8 where we read this verse, Romans 8: "For we know that all things work together for good to those who love God, those who were called according to His purpose."

Ouch. I did not even finish the chapter. I set the Bible down and held back tears. All things work together for good? Even this horrible week was working for my good? How?

My wife had not long before this heard someone else summarize this verse in a way that would forever change my perspective. She could see I was struggling in this moment and in her wisdom she knew I was about to lose it. She turned to me and with the deepest love in her eyes said to me, "It's better this way."

In the moment it was not easy to hear. In fact, it took several days of meditating on it for it to finally have its effect on me. A few weeks later when we were having a picnic in the lawn I had said, "I wish the sun were shining." To which she, again so wisely, responded, "The sun is always shining, Josh." I think she should write a book.

Over the course of the next several months this short quip of a commentary on Romans 8:28 became our family motto. I needed to hear it over and over again. Eventually I got it tattooed on my left forearm so that I would not be able to avoid it any longer. It is now my favorite tattoo and I still dwell on it often.

You may not believe the Bible. You may not have faith in what it says or believe that Jesus is the Messiah. You may be contemplating skipping to the next chapter and ignoring this religious zealot and his hope based on faith. I hope you don't, but the good news is I will likely never know, so it certainly won't hurt my feelings.

If you keep reading though, I would like to show you why I think this sort of faith is not just wishful thinking in a tooth fairy, but real substance that gives hope in difficult times. How can I take words written thousands of years ago about people I have never met and a God I cannot see physically and somehow find hope? Why not find something material and modern to put my hope in? How do I know the Bible is even true?

These are all good questions. Books have been written about such questions. I only have a chapter to try to share with you why I think this is worth hoping in, so buckle up.

I have taught many classes on the subject of Apologetics (or, how do we defend the authority and veracity of the Bible). So again, I realize that this chapter will not do justice to the enormity of the topic, however, let me give you a few brief comments on why I think the Bible is reliable.

The simplest 30,00 foot view is to use the acronym M.A.P.S. These letters stand for:

- M – manuscript evidence
- A – archeological evidence
- P – prophetic evidence
- S – statistical evidence

Of these, this particular figure from my several pages of notes stands out this month,

> *"2,000 prophecies including approximately 200 about the life, death, and resurrection of Jesus. While a few of the prophecies have not yet been fulfilled (for example, the Second Coming of Christ), there are no prophetic failures."*

In other words, when God says something He means it. He is faithful to all His promises. All of His promises are, "yes" and "amen". And in our own life we have seen this time and time again. This isn't a book on miracles, per se, so I won't go into the details of how we somehow avoided bankruptcy all three times. How we somehow paid all our bills even though the math clearly did not add up. How many times I ran those numbers and could not figure out how we did not miss a single bill during those difficult months. I may never understand how, but I know Who.

So here's the rub. All of these difficult times and the providence that shaped the life of my family over the course of 15+ years led us to the mission field. We are missionaries with an organization in South Texas and have been serving here for four years now with no plans of leaving anytime soon. My hope is found in Jesus Christ and His faithfulness to all His promises. I make no bones about it. Even in the worst of times, which we have had many, He has been faithful to all His promises and has seen us through.

God created the world and made humans in His image. A special creation out of all that was created. Humans rebelled against Him through sin and set in motion a marvelous plan of redemption wherein God would be reconciled with them. Through the course of time with many prophecies predicting events that would happen thousands of years in the future written down by many different authors from different time periods, all pointing to the redeeming work of Jesus on the cross, God brought the ultimate hope to mankind. He became human Himself to take on the sins of the world, live the perfect life we should have lived, die the horrible death we deserved to die, all to bring us redemption and peace through reconciliation with Him.

Understanding now the context of my life and the presupposition that I am using going forward, I would like to look at a few verses that bring me hope in difficult times. The first is from Psalm 130,

> 1 Out of the depths I call to you, LORD!
> 2 Lord, listen to my voice;
> let your ears be attentive
> to my cry for help.

> 3 LORD, if you kept an account of iniquities,
> Lord, who could stand?
> 4 But with you there is forgiveness,
> so that you may be revered.

> 5 I wait for the LORD; I wait
> and put my hope in his word.
> 6 I wait for the Lord
> more than watchmen for the morning—
> more than watchmen for the morning.

In my distress, anxiety, fear, loneliness, depression...I cry out to Him. I cry out to the Lord because He is the only one who has any power to rescue me. But even in this moment I am aware of my shortcomings, my sin. I realize that in my impurity I cannot stand before Him. I need to be made clean. I need to be holy. That holiness needed to stand before Him has been offered freely. In Jesus I am holy, I have been forgiven, and I can stand in the presence of God as His child, holy and blameless. Romans 8:1 says that "there is now NO condemnation for those who are in Christ Jesus."

Knowing that I have been forgiven and that I am now a child of the King. I can not only stand in His presence, but I can also cry out to Him for help. I can even complain and voice my pain and frustration like any child pleading with their dad for answers. And even more, I can wait. "I wait and put my hope in [Him]." As is often the case I do not get audible answers when I cry out in pain and even frustration. I am often reminded to simply wait and see what He is doing through this moment.

Even in the most painful and inexplicable moments of suffering I can sit patiently at His feet and wait. "Time heals all wounds" is an overused cliché that rarely brings comfort in the moment, however, there is truth there. How many times has a difficult time in your life made so much sense five years down the road? Hindsight is often enlightening in regard to difficult times.

One example of this from my own life is those early years. I didn't mention before that after our two year anniversary we filed for divorce. It was one of the most difficult times in my life. I could not even express the depths of pain that I went through during those six months. I won't get into the details of all that occured during those six months, but suffice it to say that it was a time of frustration, confusion, existential crisis, and a lot of difficult feelings.

As I now sit twenty years removed from that event I have a lot of interesting thoughts. Had it not been for that divorce (by the way, we did reconcile in the eleventh hour), there are four more children of mine that would not have been born. I can look at each of them and think, *had it not been for that difficult six months, I would have never known you. You would not have even existed.* I can also say with certainty that I would not be here writing this right now. All of our work in missions, all of our service to the church before these four years, all of the counseling sessions we led helping others reconcile marriages, would never have happened. Our lives would have taken drastically different paths. Hindsight is a clarifying tool for suffering.

I can also find hope in the promise that this life is temporary and that all things will be restored one day. Being shortsighted can often be a cause of fear in this life. When I am becoming too detail-focused I often remind myself, "One billion years from now, these few years on earth will seem so far away." Am I really going to let that guy who cut me off on the highway ruin my day? Is it really worth getting so upset because someone spilled coffee on me? Such tiny things in the view of eternity.

And this is ultimately my hope. A hope of glory. A hope of a new heavens and a new earth. Total reconciliation in Christ Jesus. Colossians 1:27, "God wanted to make known among the Gentiles the glorious wealth of this mystery, which is Christ in you, the hope of glory." Revelation 21:1-7

> 1 Then I saw a new heaven and a new earth; for the first heaven and the first earth had passed away, and the sea was no more. 2 I also saw the holy city, the new Jerusalem, coming down out of heaven from God, prepared like a bride adorned for her husband.
>
> 3 Then I heard a loud voice from the throne: Look, God's dwelling is with humanity, and he will live with them. They will be his peoples and God himself will be with them and will be their God. 4 He will wipe

away every tear from their eyes. Death will be no more; grief, crying, and pain will be no more, because the previous things have passed away. 5 Then the one seated on the throne said, "Look, I am making everything new." He also said, "Write, because these words are faithful and true." 6 Then he said to me, "It is done! I am the Alpha and the Omega, the beginning and the end. I will freely give to the thirsty from the spring of the water of life. 7 The one who conquers will inherit these things, and I will be his God, and he will be my son.

And in the midst of this current COVID-19 pandemic, things are upside down. Our ministry across the border is on pause. Our ministry is on standby just waiting to see what might come from all of this. It would be easy to think we have built all this for nothing. It would be easy to fall into anxiety, fear, or depression, worrying that what we have been called here to do cannot be done, at least for a season. But I hope.

My hope is not that I will live my best life now, here on this earth, but that all things will be made new and that we will dwell in the presence of God forever. That all pain and suffering will be gone. Every tear will be wiped from every eye. No more sadness, no more pain, no more anxiety, depression, suffering of any kind. All gone.

And that's not to say that we cannot enjoy this earth. In fact I think it is important to enjoy this life as much as possible. Visit other countries, try new experiences, find joy in the creation that is. There is no reason to spend 80 hours in the office and never get the chance to experience the joy that we can find in this world. However, I do not put my hope there. My hope is in the eternal.

I often go back to that passage in Romans and read the rest of the chapter. I know that it is better this way because He has a perfect plan and is working all things together for good, even when it doesn't make sense to me. And I can praise Him in the middle of this storm knowing that He is good. The rest of the chapter goes as follows:

Romans 8:28-39
28 We know that all things work together for the good of those who love God, who are called according to his purpose. 29 For those he foreknew he also predestined to be conformed to the image of his Son, so that he would be the firstborn among many brothers and sisters. 30 And those he predestined, he also called; and those he called, he also justified; and those he justified, he also glorified.

31 What then are we to say about these things? If God is for us, who is against us? 32 He did not even spare his own Son but offered him up for us all. How will he not also with him grant us everything? 33 Who can bring an accusation against God's elect? God is the one who justifies. 34 Who is the one who condemns? Christ Jesus is the one who died, but even more, has been raised; he also is at the right hand of God and intercedes for us. 35 Who can separate us from the love of Christ? Can affliction or distress or persecution or famine or nakedness or danger or sword? 36 As it is written:

> Because of you
> we are being put to death all day long;
> we are counted as sheep to be slaughtered.

37 No, in all these things we are more than conquerors through him who loved us. 38 For I am persuaded that neither death nor life, nor angels nor rulers, nor things present nor things to come, nor powers, 39 nor height nor depth, nor any other created thing will be able to separate us from the love of God that is in Christ Jesus our Lord.

And so I hope. No one and no circumstance can separate me from the love of God. No one can snatch me out of His hand. No one can make plans for me that go against His will or remove His power to deliver me.

Josh "Paul" and Jody Wood are missionaries with To Every Tribe in southern Texas and work to plant churches in Northern Mexico. Josh also works as the communications coordinator and helps missionaries around the world to communicate effectively with their supporters and sending churches. They have five children aged 9 to 20, one of whom lives and works in Michigan. They have been married 21 years. Josh can be reached at josh.wood@toeverytribe.org

CONCLUSION

On March 16th 2020, the President of the United States released the first in a series of coronavirus related guidelines entitled "15 days to slow the spread." Later that same day, we released the first episode of the Last Life Ever Podcast. We had been working towards a March 16th release date for almost six months. We had our first guest lined up, we were in our respective studios, ready to go live and we stopped to debate whether we should hold off, whether we should wait out the fifteen days or whether we should move forward with the live show. What we didn't yet appreciate that day is that we were in the beginning period of the biggest news story of our lives.

We chose to push forward. We do not know for sure whether we made the right choice but we do know that we have no regret. We have had great guests, who have helped us get through this challenging time. Listening to that first episode is like a time capsule into how we felt that first day. We talked about all the things we would do during our time in isolation. Jillian talked about educating her children and playing games. Jeff talked about learning a new language and working through his backlog of projects. As weeks have passed, we have shared our struggles and successes. We have tried to stay positive and share stories of light and hope with our viewers and our listeners. Six episodes in and more than a month later, as we write this, we are still under stay-at-home orders, we still have no idea when those will be lifted. We still do not know when or what our lives will look like once this period passes.

When we first talked about the idea of compiling this collection of essays, we did so in desperation. We had entered into this period optimistic and believing that it would be over soon. We had big plans for all the stuff we would get done, all the new tricks we would learn during our short break from our everyday lives but a few weeks in, we both found ourselves struggling to cope with the uncertainty. Neither of us had learned any new skills, we were both eating poorly and drinking more. We both struggled much more than either of us anticipated. That being said, while it has been hard for us, we also recognize that we are comparatively fortunate. So many people around the world have it much much worse.

This book was written and compiled for those who are struggling. This book is for all of us as we live through and ultimately reflect back on this period. Each of the authors in this collection speak for themselves. They were given the freedom to write whatever they wanted, they were simply asked to write their own experiences with COVID 19. We told them we were looking for positive stories, thoughts and strategies and we let them tell the truth that they saw. We did not know what to expect.

We were hopeful but we had no idea how much these essays would ultimately mean to us. Reading them has helped us move forward in this uncertain time. We have taken inspiration from some truly extraordinary people. We have been taught strategies to divert our focus from things we can not control towards things we can. We have learned new skills (how to read poetry, how to cook). We have learned to draw upon our past experiences and challenges. We have been challenged to dig deep within ourselves, our beliefs and our faith to find gratitude and peace. We have been given strategies on how to come out of this period a better, stronger and more complete person. But most of all we have been encouraged and filled with hope.

ACKNOWLEDGEMENTS

We would like to begin by thanking the nearly one thousand members of our, Last Life Ever Facebook group, the group is growing daily and it means a great deal to us. It is a source of constant encouragement and joy. If you are a member already we appreciate your support and if you are not yet a member, but are someone who values positivity and knows that there is more to life, then we would encourage you to join this free group. We would also like to thank everyone who contributed to the creation of this book, either directly, as in the case of the authors, or indirectly, the many people who encouraged us as we moved forward with this project. We would also like to thank all of the people who support our show, the Last Life Ever Podcast. Finally, we want to thank you, our readers. Thank you so much for reading this book we hope that you found what you were looking for. Special thanks to Brad Ball for the amazing cover art. Check him out at bradball.com

SPECIAL THANKS TO OUR AUTHORS

Pete Steadman

Diana Gipe

Frank McKinney

Erdenebuyan Enkhjargal

Pili Yarusi

Jason Miller

Karen Miller

Adam Enochs

Shandi Fortunato

Kevin Fox

Lucie Ptasznik

Marisa Wilke

Jeffrey Hank

Dr. Jean LaCour

Katie Magill

Rob Crisell

Melanie & Josh McCallen

Pete Kotman

Liz Goll Lerner

Rachel Andersen

Joanne Stark

Libby & Mike Flowers

Ryan Stewman

Nathan Fraser

Heidi Rau

Josh & Jody Wood

JILLIAN SIDOTI

I would like to thank my husband, Derek who brought me food and cleaned the house during this whole quarantine. The man is a saint. I would like to thank Tyler and Tommy, my two sons who suffered through the virus with courage and my son Nikki for continuing to make me laugh. Jeff Holst is the best partner for whom a girl could ask. This book was all his vision and he pushed me when I didn't think I could be pushed. I am so grateful for that. Finally, I would like to thank God for....EVERYTHING.

JEFFREY HOLST

I would like to start by thanking my wife, Becky, she encouraged me through out, read most of the chapters as they came in and made suggestions on how to improve my own. I would like to thank Jillian, without whom this book would not exist. Your hard work, in spite of the many challenges you faced and are facing personally is inspiring, there is no doubt that you make me a better person. I would like to again thank the authors for their part in this project. I learned so much about so many of you and I sincerely appreciate you taking the time to write for this book. I'd also like to thank the following people for their unique contributions to this book, my chapter or my mindset over the last few months: Jason Miller, Travis Bronik, Brian Levredge, Peter Kotman, Diana Gipe, David Grabiner, April Mullins, Greg and Sandy Drye, Rebecca Matthews, Robert Holst, Kate Test, Janice Holst, Jammi Holst, Randy Justus, Rick Scuitema, Jalil Isa, Brad Keller, Vanessa Torres, Steven VanCauwenbergh, Ryan Faircloth, Tim and Jennifer Broekhuizen, Richard and Joanne Holst, Cathy Crowe, Steve Smullin, Dollar Bill Kelly, Tom Leonard, John Knowles, Heidi Rau, Emily Berryman, Aria Gilchrist, Casey Gandy, Corey Kupfer, Pili Yarusi, Anette Talie, Mike Schneider, Autumn Wooten, Sam Turnipseed, Tuba Warden and Becca Lehman, I have taken inspiration from each of you over the last few months and you all have a special place in my heart.

CPSIA information can be obtained
at www.ICGtesting.com
Printed in the USA
LVHW090031251120
672633LV00008B/282